Become a marketing pro! Learn to reach 1,000,000 with your marketing

Marketing Plan & Advertising Strategy To Reach 1,000,000 People

by Alex Genadini

Become a marketing pro! Learn to reach 1,000,000 with your marketing

Copyright © 2014 Alex Genadinik

All rights reserved.

ISBN:1495453588
ISBN-13: 978-1495453588

DEDICATION

Dedicated to my mother and grandmother who are the biggest entrepreneurs I know.

CONTENTS

CHAPTER 1. MARKETING FUNDAMENTALS AND THEORY

    i. What is marketing: combination of 3 definitions
    ii. True costs of your marketing
    iii. Why choosing the wrong marketing campaign can kill a small business
    iv. Four pillars of a successful marketing campaign: scale, cost, targeting and conversion
    v. Setting goals, expectations, and metrics: KPI
    vi. Leveraging big platforms
    vii. Your sales funnel, conversion rates and a/b testing
    viii. How to get great marketing ideas with purple cow
    ix. How to create a great marketing plan
    x. Common marketing mistakes
    xi. What is direct marketing & how to do direct marketing
    xii. Should you hire a marketing agency?
    xiii. The secret of marketing success

CHAPTER 2. OFFLINE MARKETING

    i. Strengths and advantages of offline marketing
    ii. Marketing with business cards
    iii. Presenting at events
    iv. Selling in stores
    v. Selling on your own to see customer reaction
    vi. Door to door sales
    vii. Marketing with flyers
    viii. Marketing on your car or home
    ix. Leverage your local community

CHAPTER 3. ONLINE MARKETING WITH SOCIAL MEDIA MARKETING

i. Social media marketing mistakes
ii. How to do social media marketing right
iii. Facebook marketing
iv. Google+
v. Twitter
vi. Quora
vii. YouTube
viii. Podcasting
ix. The secret of large crowdsourced sites
x. Adding social sharing buttons on your website
xi. Viral coefficient: Calculate the virality of your site
xii. The net promoter score

CHAPTER 4. ONLINE MARKETING WITH SEARCH AND SEO

i. SEO tutorial
ii. Inbound marketing
iii. Keyword research for SEO
iv. Case study of SEO beyond Google
v. Content marketing strategies
vi. Blogging and guest blogging
vii. Google penalties
viii. Cases when you can dominate the top-10
ix. How to do paid search marketing (SEM)

CHAPTER 5. OTHER ONLINE MARKETING STRATEGIES

i. How to get press with 10 different ways to get press coverage
ii. Benefits of establishing a media presence
iii. Email marketing

vi. Three types of referrals you can get
v. Affiliate marketing
vi. How to sell products
vii. Mobile app marketing
viii. How to promote a local (service) business
ix. What is network marketing, and is network marketing a scam
x. Event marketing
xi. Growth hacking

CHAPTER 6. CASE STUDIES OF GROWING DIFFERENT BUSINESSES

i. Problemio case study
ii. HakaLabs case study
iii. Comehike case study
iv. Your company's case study
v. How to reach a million people

CHAPTER 7. FURTHER RESOURCES

FORWARD

The goal of this book is to make you an absolute marketing pro, even if you don't have much experience in marketing. The book starts by giving you solid fundamentals, and then refining your thinking to think like a marketing and business professional who is determined to grow their business.

My goal in writing this book was to help every business owner reach no less than 1,000,000 people with their marketing by turning them into an incredible marketer.

CHAPTER 1: MARKETING THEORY AND FUNDAMENTALS

"Whether you think you can, or you think you can't, you are right."

- Henry Ford

i. What is marketing: 3 definitions

Let's explore some marketing theory and discuss what exactly marketing is. To give ourselves a holistic view of what marketing truly is, let's take a look at it from three different angles.

First, let's examine the origins of marketing. When a person has a need, and another person provides a solution for that need, together they form a market that is made up of a solution provider and a person who needs the solution. The solution can be provided for free, or for a price, depending on how great the need is to the person who needs the solution, and the sales skills of the person providing the solution. The job of the person providing the solution is to make sure every person who needs that solution know that they can get the solution from them.

But what happens after all the people who have a need, have gotten that need solved? The person providing the solution needs to find more customers. And the person who can provide a solution begins to expand their efforts to reach more people. A part of that effort is to create a perception in people's minds that they have the need that the solution provider can solve. And that perception can be made to exist in people who don't really need that solution. This is where marketing makes the transition from someone simply providing a helpful solution to the need of another, to the big evil companies of today whose goal is to make us relentless consumers, convincing us that we need cars, gadgets, fashion clothing, travel, health products, and anything else as long as we buy their products. And that is the genealogy of how marketing evolved from the simple solution-provider relationship to the multi-billion dollar companies doing everything they can to turn us into consumer drones.

Now, let's take a look at another definition of marketing. As business owners, what marketing means to us is much simpler. Marketing to small business owners simply means all the things we do to get exposure for our business to bring in new potential clients. This definition is simple and global. Just about every business owner wakes up each day thinking about how to get clients, and increase the revenue of their business.

The third way to look at marketing is to take a look at it beyond the second way. Simply getting people to learn about your business and try to sell as much as possible to people is a limited strategy. The approach must be more holistic. For example, your customer support is marketing. Your product quality is marketing. Every single message made by the business or any employee is marketing. Everything and anything your company ever does that is in any way public is your marketing because that shapes the larger message of how your business is perceived, and what people think about it. Additionally, all of these things determine whether your customers will recommend your business to their friends. The happier you make your customers, the more likely you will be to turn them into marketers for your business because they will naturally recommend your business to their friends.

ii. The true cost of your marketing efforts

Many people think that the cost of their marketing campaign is just the dollar amount which is the cost to have the marketing message go up on whatever platform it is meant to live on. But that is not the correct way to think about the costs of the marketing efforts. The way to think about the costs of the marketing campaign is to add:

1) Dollar costs to post the message.
2) Employee salaries required to execute the marketing campaign. If a marketing campaign takes three months of work to execute, then a part of the cost is three months of employee salary.
3) Cost of the time that it takes for the marketing effort to begin bringing in clients. For example, if it takes three months before you begin to get clients, then the cost is three months of revenue that was not earned.

Think about what happens if a marketing strategy you choose does not work out. That means the cost is also all the missed revenue your business could have earned. As you can see, the true marketing costs are quite significant. We will come back to this issue throughout this book, and discuss how to deal with it.

Marketing Costs: Negligible, Expensive And Prohibitively Expensive

Most people want to promote their business for free, and explore free marketing options before they explore paid marketing options. The concept of free is very complicated when it comes to marketing because as we just saw, cost is not just the currency you pay to place the ad. Resources such as time spent on the marketing, effort of skilled labour and paid employee time are factored into your marketing costs as well. That means that there is no such thing as free marketing.

True Marketing Cost: Almost Always Expensive

Whether a business is doing online marketing or offline marketing, to truly market and promote a business well, serious long-term effort should be invested into the chosen marketing strategy. When I go over particular case studies later in this book, it will become much more clear why I consistently emphasize long-term strategies.

Bear in mind, the creative energy that will go into marketing may not deliver instant results. It may (and often does) require months of sustained effort to see significant results.

For now, let's consider a few examples. SEO (Search Engine Optimization) often takes months to show results (even if particular pages may begin ranking in Google within hours), door to door marketing takes full days of marketing of which you cannot do anything else to help your business. PR (publicity) and social media also take time until you can get press attention, or grow a large social media following.

However, there is no certainty that these marketing efforts will bring paying clients after the marketing campaigns are successfully executed. It is a very big risk for a business to invest weeks and months in a particular marketing effort without any guarantee that it will result in a sufficient number of clients in the future.

So even though particular marketing strategies may seem like they are free to implement, as you can see, the months it takes before seeing significant results is a very expensive cost which, for small businesses, is typically an order of magnitude more expensive than the dollar amount it may cost to pay for ad placement.

Some Marketing Is Prohibitively Expensive

When you try to estimate the total costs of a particular marketing campaign, try to determine whether the costs are simply expensive, or so expensive that they are prohibitively expensive. I feel that it is important to use that language because it emphasizes just how serious your marketing strategy decisions really are.

Let's take a look at a few examples of how to correctly count the true marketing cost. Let's say you are paying $1 to acquire each website visitor. It might seem expensive because the cost is per visitor (not customer), but you are actually saving quite a bit of money on having to hire a marketer since once you pay, you just get the traffic. Not much work is required to get the actual traffic. Plus you don't have to wait for months to get that traffic. If you pay, the traffic usually comes pretty quickly. So while you pay upfront, you save money on labor costs, and not having to wait a few months for the traffic to actually come. This allows you to begin measuring the effectiveness of this traffic right away. If it works well, great! And if it doesn't you didn't waste too much time or money, and you can move on to another marketing tactic which has a chance to work. This enables you to try many things in a short span of time, which is one of the best ways to find a strategy which would work well. So in this case, paying for your marketing actually made things quite cheap overall.

Where your marketing may might become prohibitively expensive is if you do not find a cost effective way to promote your business. It is OK to lose a little bit of money while experimenting and trying to identify a marketing channel that can be successful. But if you do not find a great marketing strategy, you will be left with mediocre options that won't be too effective at bringing you customers.

Sometimes Paid Marketing Is Cheaper Than Free Marketing

We just covered this topic, but it is vital that you get a deep understanding of the issues involved here. If you pay for traffic, you can usually get it quickly. And getting traffic quickly can help you understand whether that particular marketing technique will ultimately be effective. That means you can invest hours or days instead of months before you understand what you can expect from a particular marketing strategy. And that can save you a tremendous amount time and money.

Of course, if you are low on cash, actual cash may be worth more than time and effort. So paying actual cash isn't an attractive option in many cases.

Note that I am not encouraging you to pay for your marketing. This book will focus mostly on "free" marketing techniques. But I do want you have an objective sense for the true costs of marketing before we get into particular marketing strategies later in this book so that you can always get a feel for true costs rather than just the immediate dollar cost.

Negligible Costs

Some social media marketing efforts like tweeting on Twitter, pinning on Pinterest, and posting Facebook updates takes very little of your time, and is something people can do during breaks. These are the types of costs that can be considered negligible. Even if they are ultimately fruitless in most cases, there isn't much lost in pursuing those strategies.

Cost Of Choosing The Wrong Strategy

If you choose the wrong marketing strategy, an additional significant cost for it is all the revenue and new clients you missed out on during the months it took you to execute that faulty strategy, and realize that it isn't working. You may have to start all over. And that may be the biggest cost of them all. So be very careful when choosing your marketing strategy. Do what you can to ensure that you choose a correct marketing strategy. A wrong or inefficient marketing strategy can waste months of your effort.

iii. Why choosing a wrong marketing strategy can kill a small business

Marketing is the lifeline of just about any business. It is the process by which potential customers discover that business, and take the steps to becoming paying customers.

Obviously, if too few people discover a business, that business will have too few clients, and that would very likely mean too little revenue, and doom for the business.

The first 6-18 months are crucial for most small businesses. This is the make or break period for just about any type of business. There are two survival strategies businesses have when they start, and both are, for the most part, fueled by marketing.

The first strategy is to become profitable as soon as possible by doing effective marketing, reaching a high scale of potential customers, and converting enough of them into paying customers to financially sustain the business. The second way to get your business to survive is to grow fast enough to get investors interested, or get other types of outside funding.

Since a small business typically does not have money or time it can waste, it is important to choose an excellent marketing strategy right from the start in order to meet the need for growth.

If there is no growth over a period of a few months, employees begin to lose morale, the founders can lose confidence in the direction they chose, and the entire operation may begin to operate out of a sense of increased worry and anxiety from growing at a much slower pace than was initially expected. All that creates the effect of desperation which pervades many future business decisions and actions. And you do not want your business to enter that kind of a negative psychological cycle.

If the business does not begin growing, the desperation will creep into everything the business does, causing more and more short-sighted decisions. That will reflect in poorer product quality and lower customer satisfaction, which can contribute to the demise of the business.

This is why businesses should be absolutely certain that their marketing plan can be fully executed within available resources and meet the company's growth objectives.

To do this, the marketer must consider all the strengths of the business, evaluate how to take full advantage of offline and online marketing strategies, and choose upcoming marketing efforts carefully and with precision. If things go wrong for the few initial marketing campaigns, the chances of the business' survival will be greatly reduced.

iv. The 4 pillars of any marketing strategy

As we just saw, marketing campaigns are generally expensive. Even marketing that seems to be free is usually expensive.

Even if at times the actual cost to place the ad is zero dollars, the real cost of your marketing efforts is never zero. In order to justify the costs, it is absolutely imperative for businesses to plan their marketing efforts well.

While you cannot predict the future outcome of your marketing efforts, you can come close by having a deep understanding of the four factors that make up any successful marketing effort, and using that as a guide against which to test your future marketing efforts and decisions.

The four factors are scale, cost, targeting, and conversion. Let's examine these one by one, and then together.

Scale Of The People Reached

It is important for an entrepreneur to have an idea of how many people are reached by their marketing efforts. You must have a sense for whether the potential reach for a particular marketing effort will be tens, hundreds, thousands, tens of thousands of people, or more. To determine the potential scale of any marketing effort, you must understand the nature of that particular marketing effort and the platform on which it is carried out.

The marketer must understand how the platforms on which he is advertising work, and what can be expected from those platforms. If the marketing effort is simply advertising by posting a Facebook update, then in most cases, that effort will reach relatively few people even if the marketer's Facebook group has many fans. But if a big news site decides to write an article about your business, you can get tens of thousands of people to learn about your business. Scale is a very important factor to always keep in mind.

Total Cost Of The Marketing Effort

As mentioned earlier, marketing costs are not just the costs of placing an advertisement. The cost is also the time it takes before that particular marketing effort begins working and bringing you clients. So it is tricky to measure costs with precision before you implement those marketing efforts because there is always that unknown of how the marketing effort will ultimately play out. Nevertheless, you must try to get a sense for what the costs will be.

Let's walk through an example of how to understand your

true marketing costs. For our example, let's consider that you are evaluating the decision of whether to do Search Engine Optimization (SEO) marketing to get traffic from Google search. SEO campaigns can take months to show results. In this case, the costs can be:
1) Cost of the man-hours of hiring an SEO marketer, or learning how to do SEO yourself, and then doing that SEO.
2) The time it takes and the clients you didn't get before you see results from the SEO. Initial results can be seen within mere days, but it can take several months to see significant results.

That means that the costs are equivalent to months of human effort. It also means that you will have to wait for several months before you begin to get a significant number of clients. As you can see, any way you look at it, this is quite expensive.

Let's consider another example of what happens when you advertise on Twitter.
1) It takes months to build up a solid following on Twitter.
2) It takes less than a minute per tweet, but you must tweet consistently over time.
3) The results in terms of eventual generated revenue are very unpredictable on this platform. More often than not, the results in terms of revenue that you may generate are very underwhelming.

As you can see, it can often take a very short time to begin marketing your product, but it can take a very long time to market effectively and see significant results. So very often, the true cost is often the time it takes before a particular marketing effort begins being effective, which can take months of not generating revenue. We will present some case studies covering these issues in more detail later in the book.

Targeting Your Target Consumer

Reaching the correct target audience for your business is of utmost importance. Many first-time marketers and entrepreneurs assume that everyone will enjoy their product or service. But in almost all cases, that is a crucial mistake. Determining your target market is not simple. You must have a deep understanding of your product or service in order to correctly determine what kind of people will be most likely to buy and enjoy it. You also have to get to know the typical profile of those people because knowing their needs and wants will help you create a product that they want, and that pleases them. We will come back to the topic of identifying and honing in on your target consumers later in this book.

For now, consider what happens if you reach one thousand random people with your marketing. Let's say you are selling soccer equipment. If the audience that you reach is not targeted well, many of those people won't even like sports. And even the people who like sports may only like to watch, but not play. And from the people who play, only a small percentage will be soccer players. And many of the people that do like to play, and are soccer players, may simply not need the item you are selling. Even if those people do need the kind of equipment you are selling they still may not buy because they may not like your price or the colors you have available, or a number of other things. So in the end, if you do not target people well, out of the initial thousand people, you may only be reaching a handful of people who may actually be potential buyers of your product. So correct targeting is absolutely key! Consider what happens if the thousand people whom you reach are all soccer players. Many of them would probably need your product, and you can generate tens if not hundreds of sales. That is a huge difference in results which is made possible solely with proper consumer targeting.

Marketing to an audience that is not well targeted usually results in a waste of effort because you ultimately reach almost no potential buyers. Plus, it just irritates the people whom you do reach with your marketing because what you are promoting is not relevant to them. And that is bad for your brand. So make absolutely sure you are reaching your target market, and that you have identified your target market correctly.

Conversion Of Visitors To Paying Customers

Once you have reached your target market at scale, and at a reasonable cost, you must make sure that the people you reach convert into buyers or whatever action you need them to take.

The first point of contact that people make with your business is called the top of your sales funnel. It is vital to ensure that you optimize each step of your sales funnel to have as many people as possible make it through the necessary steps in your sales funnel to go from people who just learned about your business to become actual paying customers. We will cover techniques and concepts you can use to maximize your conversion rates later in this book.

Important Note

The four pillars of a marketing that we just covered, which are cost/scale/targeting/conversion must all work together to create a successful marketing campaign. If you can achieve all four of these themes within one marketing effort, most likely that marketing effort will be very successful. As things usually work out in practice, getting all four of these to work just right in a single marketing effort is quite difficult and rare. If you can get at least three of these, your marketing campaign should work out quite well. But only getting one or two of these four themes to work the way you need would probably result in disappointing results.

v. Understanding KPI (Key Performance Indicators) for your business

Every business has different metrics which it needs to track. Obviously, for most businesses, the key metrics when it comes to marketing are new customers, revenue, and eventual profit. But that is a very limited way to look at it. Let's go over some examples.

I use my YouTube channel to drive product sales and generate revenue. But before YouTube can increase product sales, my channel must itself grow inside YouTube. So for YouTube the KPIs I need to keep track of are views per day and the number of subscribers. I need to make sure that these metrics keep growing. There are other metrics which are good to track, but for simplicity's sake, let's just use these. These are the key performance indicators for tracking my growth in YouTube. For my mobile apps, the key performance indicators are the number of downloads per day, positive reviews, and the percentage of people who use the apps daily. For my website's SEO (search engine optimization) campaign, the key performance indicators are the number of people who discover the site through search each day, and who stay to browse more than just the initial page. These basic growth KPIs pave the way to the revenue and profit that you are ultimately after.

Whatever you are trying to promote, make sure that you

identify the important metrics to track, and that you are able to track the effect of your marketing efforts on eventual results and growth of those important metrics. If you can't track your KPI's, you can't tell whether your marketing efforts are having any effect.

vi. Leveraging big platforms to reach scale with your marketing

When you first open your business, your website has no visitors, and your Twitter and Facebook group accounts have almost no followers other than your friends who are just there to support you. So how do you get your marketing message across to many people? You must identify big platforms that have traffic. That traffic must be relevant to your business (your target audience). As you work on promoting your business, constantly think of strategies for how to leverage those big platforms to get people from those platforms to come to your site. Let's take a look at a few examples.

Television is the biggest platform of all media platforms. This is why companies pay millions of dollars to advertise on TV, and especially things like advertising on Super Bowl commercials. Since most small business owners can't afford to buy TV commercials, let's examine what online options are available. Obviously, the biggest online platform is Google. That is a large part of the reason why many small business owners spend so much of their available resources on trying to get traffic from Google search. The second biggest platform online is YouTube. Social media as a whole can also be seen as a gigantic entity that is made up of many large individual sites. When you start your business, even a mid-size website can seem like a big platform to you because it can drive a comparatively large amount of traffic to your new website. We will explain how you can leverage all these platforms to drive traffic to your business later in this book. For now, just keep in mind that it is imperative that you make larger websites work in your favor. They can drive hundreds, thousands, tens of thousands, or even millions of people to your business.

vii. The sales funnel, conversion rates, and A/B testing

A sales funnel is the series of steps that a person must take from the time when they first learn about your business to the point when they become a paying client. If you are not necessarily selling something, your conversion funnel is the series of steps that a new person must take from the moment they first learn about your business to "converting" to take whatever action you need them to take.

When you are marketing your business and getting the word out about your business, you probably send people to your website or a physical location. That initial point where you tell people to go is the top of your sales funnel. Once people get to the top of your sales funnel, as a business, you must have very clear goals for what you want those people to do. And your website or store must be optimized to increase the percentage of people who make it through every step of your sales funnel, and eventually perform whatever task you need them to perform.

Strategies To Improve And Optimize The Sales Funnel

If you are selling something, by improving your sales funnel you effectively increase the revenue you generate by increasing the percentage of people who convert from visitors to buyers. And that can mean the difference between life and death for a business because if you increase the rate of people who buy, that also means that you increase the average lifetime value of a customer, which means that you can spend more money to get each customer. And if you can spend more money to get each customer, more marketing options become available to you, and it becomes easier to get those customers.

Measure Everything To Optimize Your Sales Funnel

Let's say that you have a site to which you drive people, and that website is the top of your sales funnel. What you need to do is use web analytics software to measure and understand what those website visitors are doing on your site. If you are not familiar with web analytics, you definitely need to be. Look up GoogleAnalytics on the web and begin using it. It is a very popular free web analytics software, and will help your business get insight about what your website visitors are actually doing on your website.

Web analytics will help you have a better sense of what people are doing when they come to every page of your website. As far as you are concerned, you need those website visitors to go to the next step in the sales funnel from whichever page your website visitors are on. With analytics, you will be able to see whether people are making it to the next part of the sales funnel, and at what rate they are doing that. You will also get insight about what parts of your site may be causing potential customers to leave, or get stuck in the sales funnel. And once you are able to identify those problem points within your sales funnel, you will be able to eventually fix and improve those problem points.

Test Everything With A/B Testing To Optimize Your

Sales Funnel

By now you may be asking how you can increase the rate at which people move forward through your sales funnel. What you have to do is define a clear call to action (usually a big button) letting people know that this is where they need to go next on your website, and what value is in it for them.

Once you have added your call to action, try experimenting with where on that page the call to action should be, and what phrasing may work best. Different placement of the call to action, and text on and around the call to action can have a pretty significant effect on the rate at which people go to the next step in your sales funnel. And A/B testing can help you test which text and placement on the page is most effective.

A/B testing is simply the idea of creating two or more versions of a particular web page, and testing which of those versions gets a higher percentage of people doing whatever you need them to do on that page. It works hand in hand with analytics because analytics will help you understand what your website visitors are doing on each version of the page. You can continue to use A/B testing and analysing the resulting user behavior until you are happy with the percentage of people who perform the actions that you need them to perform on that page. Once you are satisfied with the conversion of that particular page, move on to optimize the conversion in the next step of your sales funnel until the entire sales funnel is maximally optimized and you have increased your site's conversion rate to a healthy point.

Create Landing Pages

Another approach to optimizing your sales funnel iis to minimize the number of steps in the sales funnel. While increasing the conversion rate of each step in the sales funnel is great, you can also optimize your sales funnel by decreasing the number of steps a person must take, down to just one step. That single step is called the landing page.

Landing pages are a great tool to help you minimize the steps in your sales funnel, and increase conversion of visitors to buyers. Landing pages are specific pages you can create on your site, which have a single and clear call to action, which is usually to move the visitor to a pretty advanced step in the sales funnel, or have them sign-up or buy something right from that page.

Once you have your landing pages pages set up, their conversion rates A/B tested, and are sure that the landing pages have a high-enough rate of conversion, you can then drive people to those landing pages. With landing pages, you can also measure success of conversion more accurately because they offer only one step, and you can set up a unique landing page for a unique marketing campaign, which will allow you to track how exactly that marketing campaign is working out. With the ability to have more precise tracking of results, methods like direct marketing become a more useful tool for you. We will cover direct marketing more fully in an upcoming section of this book.

viii. How to get great and unique marketing ideas with the purple cow

We are all familiar with good and common marketing ideas such as SEO (Search Engine Optimization), social media marketing, getting press coverage, and so on. But one thing that takes a typical good marketing idea from being simply good to being great is originality and uniqueness.

Seth Godin, who is one of the leading thinkers in marketing today, has championed the concept of the Purple Cow. Have you ever seen a purple cow? Since purple cows do not exist, I am going to guess that you have never seen a purple cow. Would you be surprised if you ever saw a purple cow? I am going to guess that you would at least give it a second look if you ever did come across a purple cow. And that unique and unexpected element is precisely the analogy that you need to bring to your marketing efforts. Let's consider an example of how I used the concept of the purple cow with one of my early businesses.

I used to organize group hikes. In the beginning, almost no one would attend my hikes because my hiking group was unknown, and I was relatively unknown. Plus, I didn't have any "large platforms" which I could leverage to get the word out about my hikes. Then I got the idea to do a very unique type of a hike. It was going to be a hunt for a shipwreck that could be seen in the water during low tide. That event theme was so unique and interesting for a hike that it immediately got the attention of the main newspaper for my city (a very large platform for me compared to any other means I had available to advertise!). The newspaper published my hike on their Sunday events section, and it drove hundreds of people to my hike. In fact, there were way too many people to actually take on a hike with me. So I had to turn many people away because I simply could not take so many people with me on a hike.

That was the difference between doing regular marketing, and spicing it up with the purple cow. Adding creativity, uniqueness, and originality got me the extra attention I needed to get extra exposure. The shipwrecks were my purple cow. You will have to think about what the purple cow will be for your business. Once you come up with a great purple cow concept that makes sense for your business, it can make a world of difference for your marketing efforts. Keep in mind that for most people, it takes time before stumbling on a really great purple cow concept for their business. It took me a while to come up with the shipwreck hike idea. But once I did, it worked magically. So don't be discouraged if you don't find your purple cow right away. Just keep thinking about what the purple cow will be for you, and it will come to you.

ix. How to create a great marketing plan

A marketing plan is a document that is internal to your company. It can be shaped over time by multiple employees. That means you don't need to focus on too much on formatting details because the document will be for internal use. But you do have to make sure that the marketing plan document outlines a marketing plan that is actually viable, and likely to be effective.

The important items that a marketing plan should cover is the time horizon for particular marketing campaigns, the target market, and the particular strategies for reaching that target market. When it comes to the particular strategies, use our "4-pillars of marketing" concept to evaluate whether each particular marketing technique you are planning to implement within your marketing plan will get you the results you are after.

Here are the typical sections of a marketing plan:

- Schedule and deadline.

- What sets your business apart from your competitors. This is how you differentiate from the competition overall, and in your marketing messages.
- The profile(s) of a target consumer that you are after with demographics and psycho-graphics (more details on this later in the book).
- Your marketing goals in terms of the scale of people you need to reach.
- List of particular techniques you will try with an evaluation of results and cost of each.
- How much money is needed to execute the plan.

x. Common marketing mistakes

While there can be many potential mistakes you can make with your marketing, there are a few mistakes which, if avoided, should ensure that your marketing campaign has a good chance to be successful.

Not Focusing On A Target Market

There will be a full section of this book devoted to correctly choosing your target market. For now, it is important to understand that if you reach people who have no need for your product, just about all of them will either ignore your ad, or get irritated with your ad, and will not buy anything. That means your marketing efforts will be wasted. When you do any kind of marketing, make absolutely sure that you will be reaching your target market, and that you have chosen your target market correctly.

Underestimating The Amount Of Work That Is Required

While all entrepreneurs hope that their marketing efforts will quickly result in amazing success, that rarely happens. In most cases, to make a marketing technique work well, you have to work long and hard at it. Yes, there can be overnight viral hits, but they are rare, and typically have strong marketing muscle behind them that we don't see as consumers. In most cases, to see significant results, there must be months of sustained hard work. Most savvy marketers and business owners will tell you that they spend a tremendous amount of time and resources on marketing whatever it is that they are selling. We will see this in the case studies presented later in this book.

xi. What is direct marketing, and how to add elements of direct marketing to your marketing campaigns

Direct marketing is generally thought of as selling something directly to the public, with the key element being reaching the consumer directly without any middlemen. Examples of direct marketing are mail order catalogues, email sales campaigns, phone sales, and similar techniques where the seller can go directly to the consumer.

The strength of direct marketing is that because the seller can go directly to the consumer, the seller can get precise sales data for the results of the campaign. For example, if 100 sales phone calls are made, and 10 sales are made during those calls, then the seller can track sales with 100% precision. The seller can also track the costs it took to generate those sales with equal precision. And that is the true value of direct marketing. Being able to track sales and costs with precision helps the marketer understand the exact costs, revenue, and profit of a particular marketing effort. Once the costs and the revenue can be precisely accounted for, there is no longer any guessing or uncertainty about whether that particular marketing effort is ultimately profitable or not.

We want to take that theme of measuring as much as we can, and incorporate that theme into all of our other marketing efforts as much as possible.

xii. Should you hire a marketing agency?

There are a number of benefits to hiring a marketing agency. They usually specialize in a particular marketing tactic like SEO (Search Engine Optimization), social media marketing, getting you press coverage, or something else. And if the agency is any good, they will often get you good results that are better than you can get on your own because they have so much more experience with the particular marketing strategy or tactic in which they specialize.

The problem with hiring an agency is that if they are any good, they tend to be quite pricey. And if they are too cheap, be careful because chances are that the quality of their work may be lacking, and you may waste your time and money with them. Nevertheless, there are many good agencies which are reasonably priced.

My preference though, is that you learn how to do marketing. The reason it is important to do your own marketing, at least in the beginning, is that it will give you a good sense of what kinds of things will work and won't work. And that comes with experience. This experience will help you come up with better and better higher level thinking and strategy for your business. Doing your own marketing will also help you to get close to your target market, and get to know them better. You must ultimately get to know your target market better than they know themselves. So anything you can do to get close to them, and observe and monitor their behavior, is extremely valuable.

My goal in this book is to empower you with enough knowledge to think through high level strategies, as well as to be able to execute on the details of particular marketing tactics. That way you will be able to save money because you will not need to hire marketing help, and will be empowered to do your marketing on your own.

xiii. The secret to marketing success

I want to finish this fundamentals of marketing chapter by covering what I feel is the one secret to marketing success. And no, this is not some get rich quick scheme where you get rich by learning this one tip for success. Or maybe it is, because my one secret to marketing success is to work very hard. That is my secret to marketing success: hard work. And I mean it. Be ready to put a tremendous, sustained long-term effort into your marketing. Few things covered later in this book will work without putting in the hard work. And if you do put in the necessary hard work into your marketing efforts, it is very likely that your marketing efforts will be successful, and you will be glad that you did.

CHAPTER 2: OFFLINE MARKETING

It is important to focus on offline marketing first because online marketing has evolved to be a much fuller and broader topic. Plus, there are very valuable elements in offline marketing that we can take with us to our online marketing efforts to make those online marketing efforts much more effective.

i. Strengths of offline marketing

There are a few elements of offline marketing that are extremely valuable, and that I want to encourage you to always keep in mind. In many offline marketing efforts, you will get the chance to meet people face to face, look them in the eyes, and have an opportunity to start a business relationship that can last for many years, and have mutual benefits far beyond simply selling them whatever you are currently trying to sell. Offline marketing gives you a chance to meet people, and with every person you meet, you get a chance to start a great business relationship.

Additionally, during your offline marketing, very often, you will get to observe how the people to whom you are trying to sell your product actually interact with your product when they first come in contact with it. You can observe their facial expressions, get feedback about the product right on the spot, and ask those people questions about what they truly think about your product.

There is a theme here. Your offline marketing strategies have a much richer human component than your online marketing strategies. And that is something very valuable to always keep in mind.

Of course, the weakness of offline marketing is that it does not scale well since we can't start personal relationships with thousands of people each day.

ii. Marketing by handing out business cards

Handing out your business cards can be a good way to help you market your business. Although most of the time, you might exchange business cards with people at business networking events, always carry business cards with you wherever you go. You never know when casual conversation may turn to business, and you can use that opportunity to segue into talking about your business.

Marketing with business cards is good for two reasons. The first reason is obvious in that the person to whom you are giving the business card may visit your website or store, and become a client of your business. But the second reason that handing out business cards is great is that exchanging business cards gives you a chance to stay in touch with the person to whom you gave it, and potentially form a business relationship with that person. And that business relationship can be mutually beneficial for a long time.

Following Up After The Business Card Exchange

Whenever you take someone's business card, it is easy to just put it in your pocket, forget about it, and never follow up because the business cards tend to get lost and forgotten if they just lie around somewhere. But that is unprofessional. Proper business card exchange etiquette is to make sure that you follow up and email everyone whose business card you took. Preferably, follow up during the very next day or two. That shows people that you are dependable, serious, and reliable. When you are marketing your business by handing out business cards, it is equally important to follow up with the person after the event, as it is to make the initial connection.

Make Notes Right After Exchanging The Business Cards

It is good practice to carry a pen with you when you go to networking events. That way, you can make quick notes on the back of the business cards that you collect. That helps you remember the important topics that you just discussed with the person whom you met. It always feels like you will remember all the details of the conversations you have, but in practice, after a day or two, we tend to forget many details about our conversations, especially if we collected many business cards that day. Making a few notes on the back of the business cards right after you initially chat with a person, will help you remember this particular person and the main points of the conversation about which to email.

Ask How You Can Help

When you meet people, it might be tempting to talk to them about your business, and to try to get them to become customers of your business. And you should probably do that at some point. But it is always good to ask the people you meet about what they are working on, and try to see whether you are able to help them in any way. If you offer help or kind words, people will be more inclined to be interested in your business, and would also be more motivated to help you. So before you talk about your own business and hand someone your business card, make sure to ask that person about what they are doing, and try to get genuinely interested in their work. Remember, that kind of reciprocity is a great foundation for any kind of a relationship, whether it is a business or a personal relationship.

Marketing With Business Cards Does Not Scale

The drawback of marketing with business cards, like many other offline marketing techniques, is that it does not scale. There are just not that many people you can talk to and build relationships with because each such relationship is relatively time consuming. In the next section of the book, we will go over how to add scale to your business card marketing efforts by becoming the center of attention at networking events.

iii. Marketing by presenting at events

Networking at business events is great. But being the presenter at business events is far better. By speaking at the event, you will be able to get the message out about your business to everyone in attendance. The theme of the evening will revolve around your business, and you will be the center of attention. After your talk, many people will come up to you, and talk to you about your business. Plus, speaking at events has many additional benefits.

When you are running your business, you always want to position yourself as the thought leader in your business niche. One great way to do that is to speak at events. You might not only get clients from the people who are in the audience, but there may be some bloggers or journalists in the audience. And if they like what you are doing with your business, you may get extra coverage in the publications for which they write. Try to talk to as many people as possible after your talk, give out business cards, and don't forget to always ask what the people you talk to are doing, and how you can help them with whatever they may be working on. Don't just focus on your own sales.

iv. Selling your product in brick & mortar stores

Another offline marketing strategy in the theme of leveraging large existing platforms, is to get physical stores to sell your products if the products that your business makes are something that can be sold in stores or physical locations.

The stores already have shoppers. All you have to do is get the stores to sell your products. The kinds of things you can sell in stores range from food to clothing to handmade items to toys or souvenirs, to many other kinds of items. In most cases, all you have to do is walk into the store and ask them about the process of getting something sold in their store. If it is a big store or a large chain, very likely they already have a set process for small businesses who want to sell their products through their stores. If the store is a mom and pop store, or a business that has just one location, very likely the owner of that store is actually in the store during business hours so you can engage in conversation with them just by walking in.

Keep in mind that selling in big stores is very difficult because not only do they have a lengthy application process, but even if they decide to sell your items, they may buy your products at a very low price and impose a number of restrictions on packaging and other issues. For many small businesses, that often means losing money in exchange for the big-store exposure. If you are not a big brand, you just don't have the negotiating leverage, and big stores typically use that to their advantage.

v. Selling your products on your own

If your product is something that can be physically sold by exchanging it for cash, just like it might be in a brick & mortar store, you can also sell that product at flea markets or from carts, or stands. Yes, that is not sexy, and it can feel intimidating. But there is an amazing benefit to doing this. First, you might make some money by selling your product this way. But the amazing benefit you gain from this experience is that you will be able to observe how people react to your product, its price, and how they interact with it. It will also give you a chance to talk to those people, and ask them questions about what they think about your product, and what may be preventing them from making a purchase. Once you get that feedback, you can improve your product to no longer have the weaknesses noted by the people you talk to, and go back out to sell the product again. Doing that multiple times will help you greatly improve your product, which will help you improve sales wherever you will be selling it in the future.

vi. Door to door sales

Door to door sales is not too effective for most businesses, but there are some types of businesses for which it can be very effective. For example, if your business is a home painting business, you can literally walk around affluent neighborhoods (because those neighborhoods have people who could afford various services) and knock on doors of homes which have aging or old paint jobs. In many cases, the homeowners probably already know that they need to get a new paint job, and will actually be glad that you stopped by because they may have been procrastinating on hiring painting contractors to help them paint their home. You can leave them your business card, brochure, and pricing information. If they need this kind of a service, they may give you a call.

vii. Marketing with flyers

Passing out flyers is less personal than giving people your business card because there is no conversation that ensues before or after the flyer exchange. And many people simply glance at the flyer and throw it away. Nevertheless, most first-time marketers have a marketing plan that goes something like "I will promote my business by handing out business cards, flyers, and promote my business on social media sites like Facebook and Twitter." So passing out flyers is one of the initial strategies for many first-time marketers and first-time entrepreneurs. Let's give this strategy some attention.

How To Design The Flyers

There are a few important elements that make or break a flyer marketing campaign. One important thing to keep in mind is that when you hand out flyers to people, those people are usually on the go. That gives you only a few seconds during which they glance at your flyer before they even determine whether they will even take it from your hand, and whether they will take a closer look at it, or throw it away (hopefully they will recycle the flyer instead of throwing it into the garbage).

That means that you have to display the value proposition in big letters, and clear print. What you are promoting should be immediately clear on your flyer, and it should also be clear what the value is for the person looking at the flyer. Is there a discount? Or an interesting event? That has to be clear from the initial glance at the flyer.

Additionally, try to not go too heavy on the graphics. While graphics can be enticing and alluring, they can also cause a little bit of confusion during the few seconds during which the person to whom you are giving the flyer is trying to decide whether they will take it or not. Try to have clear images that add to the flyer's message, without making the flyer layout confusing or cluttered.

Cost Of The Flyers

Marketing your business with flyers isn't free. In fact, printing the flyers isn't very cheap. A low quality flyer can cost a few cents to print, and a high-quality flyer can cost nearly a dollar to print. As you might guess, cheap flyers will get you the kinds of results that you paid for. So you will have to give out more flyers and spend more time giving out those cheaply made flyers, which makes them less cheap overall. Additionally, if you hire someone to hand out the flyers, that is an additional cost as well.

To fully understand how many passed out flyers it takes you to get a single customer, you must be able to determine whether the flyers generated any leads. That means that the contact information on those flyers must be unique. It can be a unique phone number or a url that people should visit. That will help you measure how many people contacted you after they got your flyers. Think back to our theme of using elements of direct marketing. You must have some way to measure the effectiveness of your flyer-marketing efforts. Even if people walk into your business, if you can, try to ask them where they learned about your business so that you can gauge which of your marketing efforts are bringing in the most clients. Sometimes having a coupon printed right on the flyer will get the customer to bring in the flyer when they come in. And that will help you determine whether the flyers were effective at bringing you clients, and how many customers the flyers helped to bring in.

Make Sure You Reach Your Target Market

When you are doing any kind of marketing, make sure that you do not waste and mis-direct your marketing efforts. That means that you have to reach your target market with your efforts. When it comes to marketing your business with flyers, that means handing out the flyers in places where you are most likely to reach your target audience. As much as possible, try to take out randomness out of who gets your flyers.

viii. Marketing on your own print media

If you are resourceful, there is (almost) no limit to the kinds of things on which you can print your company's logo, phone number, or URL. You can print and wear t-shirts or hats that have your logo and URL. You can get an ad of your business printed on your car. You can create an ad on your home window. You can print many t-shirts and hats with your company's name and URL on them. Some of these things may seem silly or "too much" but if you really want to reach as many people as possible, these are very viable options.

In a similar pattern, you don't need to limit these kinds of marketing efforts to properties that you own. You can get other businesses and people to help you. One way to do that is by leveraging the power of your local community.

ix. Leverage your local community

There is a lot of potential in getting your local community behind you, and supporting your business. For different people, their local community can be something different. For some people, it is their religious group. For others it is their minority group. Yet for others, the local community may be the community of people who are the target market of their business because they share similar interests. For example, if your business sells soccer supplies, you probably enjoy soccer yourself. And all the local soccer leagues and players are your community and your target market at the same time. Try to find ways to get the community to rally, and support your business. If you can accomplish that, the benefits can be unending.

x. Your own event series

As mentioned earlier, it is great if you can present your business at events. The problem is that there are not that many events at which you can regularly present. So why not create your own event series? Your event series can have something to do with the theme of your main business, which will mean that the people who attend your events will also be the target consumers of your main business.

Having your own event series can help you promote your business, earn money directly from event attendees, establish many business relationships, and be at the center of the event every single time.

Additionally, if your event series works out, you can put on events on a regular basis, which will give you the ability to promote your business that way regularly. Later in this book we will have tutorials and case studies on how to put on a successful event series and promote events.

CHAPTER 3: ONLINE MARKETING USING SOCIAL MEDIA

Social media is different to everyone. Almost every communication platform that offers communication to more than two people at the same time can be considered a form of social media. For ordinary people, it is a way in which they can access news and information, and communicate with friends and family anywhere in the world. For business owners it is a platform to communicate with existing and potential customers, and to boost brand awareness and sales.

For marketers, it is a space of enormous potential due to the sheer scale of social media. Almost everyone on the web participates in social media in some capacity. And as marketers, we would be remiss if we didn't try to promote our business to all those people.

Wikipedia defines social media as "media for social interaction, using highly accessible and scalable publishing techniques."

This chapter will delve into what exactly is social media marketing, and how to get the most out of it for your business by creating an amazing social media marketing strategy for your business.

i. Social media marketing mistakes

As mentioned earlier, most first-time entrepreneurs or first-time marketers have as their initial marketing plan something like "I will promote my business with business cards, flyers, Facebook and Twitter." Those same marketers tend to also hope to get likes and retweets in naive hopes of growing their business through social recommendations, and having their business go viral. That means that half of their entire marketing strategy relies on social media.

That social media marketing strategy of simply pushing your marketing message out to your immediate network is what this chapter will try to get you to leave behind. There are almost too many things wrong with that method to list. Some of the problems with that social media marketing strategy is that it doesn't leverage full potential of social media, and it will likely annoy your social media contacts because they do not want to be directly sold to. Plus, it is simply ineffective at getting you the sales you are after. And that is just the tip of the iceberg when when it comes to explaining why this isn't a good social media marketing strategy.

The rest of this chapter will focus on helping you create an amazing social media marketing strategy which should get you massive exposure, clients, and set your personal and business brand above the rest.

ii. How to do social media marketing the right way

Let's take a step back, and take a look at what you can accomplish with social media at a high level before we dive into the specifics of how to actually get clients with social media marketing.

First, it is important to establish that social media marketing is something that is far broader than just using "social media websites" like Facebook, Twitter, Pinterest, or any other similar site. Blogging and publishing is also a form of social media. And while we are on the topic of publishing content, publishing does not have to be restricted to only publishing written content. YouTube and podcasting gives us open platforms to publish video and radio-like content. All that allows us to see social media as something that is far broader than simply writing promotional messages on our social network sites.

With the ability to reach millions of people through social sites, video, online radio, and written online publications, you can use social media to grow your personal and business brand to establish yourself as a thought leader and a visionary in your business niche. I realize that might sound intimidating. But your brand must become an authority (or one of the authoritative voices) in your business space. That will position you above the noise of all the mediocre marketers, and help your business stand out. The more you are perceived as an authority and a thought leader in your space, the more people will seek out you and your business, and engage with you and your business. Additionally, being seen as an authority will give you more trust. And having people's trust is a very important ingredient to making sales.

Let's stop for a second to take a look at what we just covered. If you establish a YouTube, podcasting, and blogging presence for your business (it is far easier than you might think. We will cover that soon), it is almost the same as getting large press coverage for your business every day since social media gives you the opportunity to establish a very strong media presence for your business.

Instead of getting press coverage for your business every rare once in a while, you would now get the equivalent of that daily, through your media channels such as YouTube, podcast, and blog. Plus, that media presence would grow along with your business over time.

This is a paradigm shift. This takes your business away from depending on other press sources to get you publicity and press coverage to giving yourself the equivalent of press coverage every single day! We will come back to this idea multiple times throughout this book because this is a one of the most powerful concepts in your marketing strategy. Now, just as you looked to other companies to give you press and exposure, other companies will look at your company to give them press and exposure. And that opens up a tremendous number of options.

SEO Benefits Of Social Media Marketing

If you think that this is where the benefits of social media marketing come to an end, there is another great side effect to establishing a strong media component in your business. That benefit is in SEO (search engine optimization). Our entire next chapter is devoted to search engine optimization so for now we just want to point out that while creating all that media, and being promoted by your promotional partners, there will be many links on different social sites, blogs, and publications that will point to your site. And all those links and people sharing those links will give you a natural SEO boost which will increase your traffic even further.

Social Media As A Networking Tool

The other way to use social media to market your business is to use it for networking. You can network with journalists and bloggers who write about your business niche. You can also use social media to network with your business peers. People are very accessible on social media and you can take advantage of that.

Leverage Influencers

An additional way to use social media is to leverage individuals and organizations who already have large social media followings (remember the theme of leveraging large platforms?). This would happen naturally as you grow your business and establish yourself and your business as an authority in your field. As you become bigger and grow your media channels like YouTube, podcast or your website, bigger players will be more inclined to get on your good side, partner with you and promote your business. Obviously you should be open to doing the same for them. And as we just covered, as you grow the media part of your business, other businesses would have incentive to leverage your business as the bigger platform which could send them traffic. So instead of you reaching out and desperately asking others to help promote your business, other businesses and individuals would be coming to you, asking for help. And that would give you the option to partner with larger and larger businesses to cross promote.

Additionally, remember that there are more social media sites than you can advertise on effectively. So choose the social media platforms on which the type of business you are trying to grow would find a natural audience, and give those social media sites your focus. Often, if you focus on fewer platforms, but establish a bigger presence on the platforms you choose, that strategy can yield better results than establishing a small presence on many social media sites. Why this is the case will be more clear when I present examples of actual case studies for how to do this type of marketing.

Marketers vs. Regular Users

First and foremost, people use social networks to interact with friends, discover interesting content, and entertain themselves when they need a break. When people engage with you on social media, it is important to remember not to be too pushy, and not to be in complete sell mode. Don't forget to be human.

As a brand, it is vital to earn and maintain the trust of your users. If people perceive you as a thing that tries to constantly sell to them, they will simply stop paying attention to you. So don't forget to always bring some value to the table.

Social media was not designed for sales or marketing. Business owners have to understand that all they can do is entice people by being interesting and engaging, and hope that a percentage of those engaged people will convert to customers in the long run.

Social Media ROI

Social Media ROI (return on investment) is the financial measurement of a business' social media advertising campaign success. In recent years, the topic has caused significant debate because big companies invest in seemingly ineffective social media marketing strategies (see posting updates on Facebook and Twitter) that don't result in new clients, but do result in spent/wasted budgets.

If you use social media marketing as it is described in this section of the book, quite likely, social media marketing will be one of the top drivers of revenue for your business. But yes, it will take up a lot of your resources (time and money) to establish a strong social media presence. But so will many of the other marketing strategies.

iii. Facebook marketing

Marketing on Facebook is the first thing every new or beginner marketer thinks of, and wants to try. So let's cover it first. There are a number of ways you can promote your business on Facebook. You can post promotional messages right to your friends, create Facebook groups or fan pages for your business, and use Facebook's paid marketing options to try reaching your target consumers. You can also encourage people to share your business on their Facebook wall which would give your business exposure to all their friends.

Posting Marketing Messages To Your Immediate Friends

The simplest way to market on Facebook is to simply post marketing messages right to your friends. This will result in some engagement because your friends trust you, and they will be curious about what you are promoting. Just don't keep promoting that same thing to your friends every day because it will simply irritate most of them and you will lose their trust. No one likes friends who try to sell things to them. It feels disingenuous.

Creating Facebook Groups Or Fan Pages

Creating Facebook groups or fan pages for your brand is a way to have a place where you can promote your work without annoying your actual friends. And the people who join and like those pages are people who want to get updates from you, and opt into it. Those could be your existing customers who want to keep in touch and get updates (this is good because you may be able to sell more to them, and they might recommend your brand to friends), or potential new customers. The problem most small businesses encounter is that it is difficult to grow a substantial Facebook group audience from scratch. Even once you do create a big enough Facebook group, Facebook does not actually show your updates to all the members of that group. You actually have to pay to reach your entire group. Does that sound sleazy on the part of Facebook to do that? It is extremely sleazy and this has been a topic of a lot of controversy. Nevertheless, that is how their platform works. That in itself is a strong argument not to over-invest in your Facebook group.

Just to make sure that you are clear on how this is sleazy on Facebook's part, let me explain again. If you make a status update on your group page which has your fans, Facebook only shows that update to about 10-20% of the people there. You would think that Facebook should show your update to your entire group, but it doesn't. To reach more of the people who already joined your Facebook group, Facebook requires you to pay each time you want to reach all the people who are in your group. And that is the case for every one of your group status updates, which for most small businesses is just ludicrous.

Paying Facebook To Target New Potential Customers

Due to the reasons mentioned above, "free" Facebook marketing has become quite tough and ineffective for many small businesses. Nevertheless, Facebook has over a million users, and we certainly want to reach many of them with our marketing message.

One reasonable option to advertise on Facebook is to pay Facebook to reach new potential customers. If you pay, Facebook provides you with targeting options like people's hobbies, interests, geographic location, education, and other information by which you can target potential new customers. Facebook's ad platform uses a pay per click model. That means you pay every time someone clicks on, or likes whatever you are promoting. The cost of the click varies on the industry in which you are in. The typical range per click is $0.05-$5.00.

Note that this is not the same as paying Facebook to make sure that your update is seen by all the members of your group. This is the option to create your own ad on Facebook which can attract new Facebook users to your group or your product. If you target people well with the targeting tools Facebook provides its paid advertisers, this option can be quite effective.

Case Study Of Problemio Facebook Marketing

Problemio.com's (my mobile app company) Facebook group, at the time of writing this book, is between 500-600 people. That isn't a big group, but it is big enough to determine how effective it might be if it grew bigger. It wasn't easy to grow this group to be this size. I had to funnel my mobile app users to like my group on Facebook. So that was expensive because I could have funneled my app users to perform another action that may have been more beneficial to my business. Nevertheless, this was a worthwhile experiment.

The engagement on Problemio's Facebook group is quite poor. As a group creator, I am able to see statistics of how many people see my status updates. Out of the 500-600 group members, only 15-50 people see my updates. That is atrocious. It is also very difficult to track sales that come from Facebook, but evidence shows that the sales from Facebook have been so low that they can almost be considered non-existent. As a business, Problemio stopped investing in the growth of its Facebook group, and makes only very infrequent updates. Instead, Problemio shifted focus to other social media platforms which we will cover shortly. Additionally, because Problemio sells mobile apps which range from $0.99-4.99 that gives very little room in terms of spending to advertise the products. For that reason it did not make financial sense to try Facebook's paid marketing option.

iv. Google+ marketing

Google+ is a social network that is a part of Google. The biggest part of Google's business is search and the monetization of search. So social networking doesn't initially seem like Google's area of concern. But in the past, Google has often stated that a strong social media presence is a positive SEO factor. That means that your website will come up higher in search results if it has a strong social media following. And since Google's foray into social media is precisely with Google+ this means that as marketers, we must pay very close attention to how this social network evolves, and Google's official statements on it. This social network is quite new, and Google itself is figuring out how to best use it within the rest of its business. So watch for changes because significant changes in how this social network really works are quite frequent.

Google+ Authorship

Adding yourself as an author may directly help your website rank better. Google has wavered on this issue on the past. Yet there is also an indirect way Google+ authorship may help your website get more traffic from search.

If you sign up for Google+ authorship (and implement it correctly), Google will place your thumbnail picture next to your URL in Google's search results. That means you will have a higher click-through percentage than if Google just listed your URL, title and page description. So even if your ranking in search results doesn't change, the click-through of your listing wherever will increase when your website does show up in search results, thereby bringing you more traffic.

As a small case study example, a few days after connecting my GlowingStart.com blog to a Google+ account for authorship, the pages of the GlowingStart.com website that showed up in search results were listed next to a thumbnail image from Google+ which resulted in slightly more traffic within just a few days.

Marketers Should Use Google+

Companies that produce and market content use Google+ as one of the platforms on which they distribute their content. One of the most appealing features of Google+ for marketers has proved to be the SEO boost. But there are a number of other benefits to using Google+. GoogleHangouts is proving to be a powerful community feature from which you can create videos that can be posted right on YouTube. And that is a good segue to underline an important point. Google is everywhere. They have leading products like Android, search, Gmail, Chrome browser, and many more. And Google users have a single account which works on all those platforms. And those platforms are tied together by

Goolge+ which means that using Google+ to at least some capacity is almost inescapable if we want to promote our products.

v. Twitter marketing

Twitter is the most open and serendipitous of all social networks. Twitter has always been the most mysterious of social networks because so many people still say that they "don't get it." It is also the one social network with the most hidden gems in terms of marketing possibilities because of its accessibility and openness.

Twitter Marketing Is Not About Immediate Selling

Like many other social networks, Twitter was not made for marketers to push their marketing messages onto people. In fact, Twitter is made to help people avoid marketing noise, and discover great content by allowing people to easily choose which accounts to follow, and un-follow if those accounts drop in quality. There is pressure on people to constantly provide great information, which in turn means that there is a wealth of great content and intelligent people you can discover on Twitter. So Twitter is a news, content discovery, and education site, first and foremost. And if you can enlighten people in some way, and establish yourself as a unique and authoritative voice within your industry on Twitter, people will follow you on Twitter, and that is when you will be able to market to people on Twitter effectively. Additionally, Twitter is quite good for business networking because almost every thought leader is on Twitter. And everyone on Twitter is always just one tweet away.

Use Twitter To Build And Maintain Business Relationships

Twitter is great for starting and maintaining business relationships. Make sure that you follow people you can learn from, your business peers, potential investors, top people in your niche, and bloggers and journalists who cover your industry. Use Twitter to keep your business contacts on your radar, and to stay on their radar. Also, try to retweet others as a courtesy. It is a small gesture, but people appreciate when you retweet whatever they are promoting, making them more likely to be responsive to you whenever you need any kind of help.

Tip: Twitter users prefer to engage with other people rather than brands. By adding the human element to your profile by being friendly and approachable, you will get more users to interact with your business. So add a picture of you to your personal account, and not of your brand logo. Plus, make your short bio description interesting and engaging.

It Is Difficult To Sell On Twitter

A common marketing mistake made by business owners on Twitter is trying to sell their products too early. This approach often fails because users are not on Twitter to shop. They are in search of good content, news, or entertainment. A long term strategy for start-up owners should be to use Twitter to build relationships, learn from others, and eventually position themselves as experts in their industry which would help them gain the trust necessary to sell on a platform like Twitter.

If you follow the long-term strategy of establishing yourself as a credible voice on Twitter, and sharing interesting content, this approach will entice users to follow the developments of your business, and become generally curious about your business. This strategy may not drive sales immediately, but it is the only viable marketing approach that could boost the brand awareness of the business being promoted.

Position Yourself As An Expert

One great strategy to get people to pay attention to your tweets, and to grow your following on Twitter is to position yourself as an expert in your niche. For example, if you are trying to sell designer clothes that you made, people would not buy your clothing if you simply post about them on Twitter. There is just no reason for people to do that. They probably don't know much about you as a retailer, and if they were looking for designer clothing, why would they not just buy from a more established business?

But if you tweet interesting things about fashion and design, and people learn from you about fashion, and retweet you because you post something of value and interest, then you can grow your following and, over time, become one of the respected voices in your niche. Once that eventually happens, you may be able to generate some sales from your Twitter followers because your voice within the industry will be more recognized, authoritative and credible.

Ineffective Twitter Strategies

There are a couple of popular strategies to grow the number of your Twitter followers, that are effective at getting more followers without truly helping your voice stand out from the crowd on Twitter, and I want to take a moment to point those out.

Many people follow everyone who follows them. And that "follow-back" strategy helps you grow your list of followers, but those followers will be worthless because they are not interested in your business. They are just interested in increasing their own follower numbers. And because they follow so many people, they can't even keep up with all the tweets from the people whom they follow. So your tweets won't even be read.

The same is true for buying Twitter followers. Yes, you can buy thousands of Twitter followers for just a few dollars. They are "bot" accounts that are not even human, and obviously won't read your tweets or engage with your business. But they will make the number of followers you have, appear to be bigger. And having a large number of Twitter followers (others won't know that most of them are fake) may make you appear as an authoritative account to follow for new people who discover your Twitter account because those new people will see your large number of followers, and wonder what is so special about you that you have so many followers, and follow you out of that curiosity.

The best way to increase your following on Twitter is to post and share interesting content and opinions that others can benefit from. Additionally, generate buzz and mentions of your business across different websites on the Internet, and then direct people from those sites to keep in touch with you on Twitter. This way you will grow your Twitter followers slowly, but they will be quality followers who will pay attention to your tweets.

vi. Quora marketing

Quora.com is a social media website where people can ask questions and get them answered by other users. Quora.com isn't as well known as Twitter, Facebook or YouTube, but it is quite powerful.

Anyone can ask or answer questions on Quora. Quora allows people to post questions about various topics and those who are knowledgeable about the particular subject matter being asked, may provide free expert answers. The experts answer questions either because they are looking to help others, or to gain something from answering. Often, the experts are marketing themselves or their businesses.

Quora marketing can help you do two things. It can help you establish yourself as more of an authority in your niche. Quora can also help you drive traffic to your site through links you post in the answers that you provide.

Positioning Yourself As An Expert Using Quora

Quora is one of the social media sites where a person can build their reputation as an expert on a topic. By providing great answers to questions on Quora, you can position yourself as an expert in your niche, gain a following, as well as increase the visibility for your business.

The value of being or seeming to be an expert is that through all the social media marketing noise and chatter, people look for leaders and experts in a niche as definitive voices. Becoming an expert could help your business attract a larger social media following of people who will listen to what you have to say more closely, and who are more likely to engage with what you are promoting or discussing. Additionally, providing great answers on Quora, and helping people, can also make you and your business more affable and likable. People will simply appreciate that you took the time to answer their questions. If people see you positively, they will be more likely to visit your site or any links you post, and possibly become customers of your business.

Quora Can Drive Significant Traffic To Your Site

Google ranks large and authoritative websites higher in search results. Quora is one of those sites that has many pages ranking in Google's top-10 search results for many different searches. When a question is asked on Quora, the page on which that question is asked (including your answer) may end up ranking in Google for some search terms. If that page remains in the top ten search results on Google searches, that could result in a constant trickle of traffic to your site over a long period of time if you included a link to one of your resources (most often some page on your website) in your answer.

If you spend enough time answering Quora questions, some of those answers will end up ranking in Google, and can give you a long-term boost in traffic.

As a case study example, I answered over one hundred questions on Quora on different topics, promoting different websites. That resulted in about 50 people *each day* coming from Quora to the sites I promoted. Since Quora drives visitors daily, over the course of a year that means 18,250 visitors! And that traffic doesn't stop coming after a year. As long as your answers rank well on Quora, they get good exposure and work to bring traffic to your website. And that can go on for multiple years as long as the question you answered in Quora keeps getting exposure, and ranking either inside Quora, or Google searches.

Tip: When you can, add links to your website or other resources when you answer questions on Quora. If you don't add a link, there is a very small chance that the person reading your answer will actually visit your site. They just won't know that you want them to visit your site.

vii. YouTube marketing

YouTube is an amazing platform for more reasons than we will be able to list here. It is the most versatile social network because its videos can live on other sites, mobile apps, and just about anywhere else. Additionally, YouTube may just be the future of television as we know it. And there is no better platform than television. Plus, YouTube gives us a chance to make as close to a personal connection as possible with our potential customers because they get to see us on video, hear us, and get to know us. That personal connection is one of the core strengths of offline marketing (remember this from the offline marketing chapter?) and thanks to YouTube, we don't have to lose that personal touch in our online marketing. There are even more benefits to YouTube marketing than that, so let's cover some of them in more detail. But before we delve more into how great YouTube is, let's explore some psychological barriers that most people have, which prevent them from taking full advantage of YouTube.

Psychological Barrier To Being A Producer

While most people have no problem with creating content like blog posts or written articles, very few people see themselves as video producers and creators. It just isn't part of our general education, nor is it a part of something we regularly do. So there is a psychological disconnect with what is possible. But chances are that you are more talented than most of Hollywood actors. With a little practice and motivation almost anyone can be a great amateur video producer. And for YouTube, that is enough to get quite far.

I can share a story from my personal experience with YouTube. Before starting my own YouTube channel to promote my mobile apps, I never had an interest in creating videos or starring in videos. And I never saw myself as being able to promote my business on YouTube. It didn't even occur to me.

But it was surprisingly simple to overcome that barrier once I realized how much YouTube can benefit my business. I will admit, in the beginning, I was absolutely terrible at video production, and starring in my own videos. But just like anything else, if you spend time on something, you become better at it. Over time, I slowly improved. I still can't say that I am any good, but I became just good enough to grow my channel, and get that YouTube channel to help market and grow other parts of my business. If you have doubts about yourself as a video producer or a star, just look at my early videos on my channel. You can't possibly be any worse. Here is the link to my YouTube channel with all my 300+ videos there:
http://www.youtube.com/user/Okudjavavich

But, of course, if you just can't get there psychologically or due to being private and not wanting to be seen on YouTube, you can get someone on your team to be in charge of YouTube production and marketing. Or in the worst case, outsource it (expensive).

Low Competition

Precisely because most people and most companies don't see themselves as video producers, they don't invest in growing their presence on YouTube, and that opens up an opportunity for you.

Don't get me wrong, YouTube is very competitive. But it would be literally hundreds of times more competitive if people and companies didn't have that psychological barrier which simply prevents them from realistically pursuing YouTube as a viable marketing option. Relatively speaking, for being the second biggest search engine in the English speaking world, and one of the most highly visited sites in the world, YouTube has relatively low competition.

YouTube Versatility

YouTube videos don't just live on YouTube. A single video can live on YouTube, and at the same time be embedded on your site, enhancing the quality of the page it is on. That same YouTube video can be added inside an app, increasing the time people spend on your app (a ranking factor in mobile app stores). The audio from that video may even be re-purposed and made into a podcast episode (more on podcasting a bit later).

YouTube Ranking in Google

My favorite thing about YouTube is that Google puts some YouTube videos in the Google search results in addition to having the YouTube video live on YouTube. That means that a single YouTube video that you create can appear in both, YouTube searches, and Google searches. And since Google is the biggest search engine in the world, and YouTube is the second biggest search engine in the English speaking world, that presents an amazing opportunity for you as the creator of that video to get exposure on these two gigantic platforms.

YouTube Is Your Media Channel

Just like you search for places where you can get exposure for your business, so do most other business owners. And other business owners will see your YouTube channel as a place where they can get exposure for your business. That puts you in a position of power and in a position to get favors from others. For example, you can invite journalists or other business owners to be guests on your YouTube channel. Doing that will help you establish a business relationship with them and make them more likely to promote you via their marketing channels as well.

Still don't think of yourself as a video creator after reading about all these potential benefits of marketing your business with YouTube? I encourage you to give it another thought.

viii. Marketing by hosting your own podcast

Just about everything we just covered about YouTube marketing is true for podcasting. Although podcasting is even less competitive. Podcast episodes can also be embedded on your website or mobile app. They are also useful for helping establish your business as an authority in your business niche. They are also effective at making a personal connection with your audience, a number of whom may at some point become clients.

If your YouTube show is a talk show like mine, you can just take the audio from your YouTube videos, and make those audio files into podcast episodes. So with very little extra work, you will have your own podcast. The two biggest podcasting platforms are iTunes and Stitcher. By hosting your own podcast, you will be able to get distribution on iTunes and Stitcher, further adding to the exposure of your business on large platforms.

ix. The secret of large-volume,

search-based sites

We can go on, listing an infinite number of social media sites and explaining their benefits and tactics for how to get ahead on such sites. But instead of doing that, let me explain the key to becoming dominant on most sites like the ones we just covered.

Notice a pattern on these sites. They are great because people just like you produce great content that is distributed on those sites. That is true for YouTube, podcasting platforms, Quora, and even Google search itself (how useful would Google be if there were no websites to search).

So what do these sites all have in common? They are all search-based, crowd-sourced sites where the crowd creates the content. Let's stop to have an a-ha moment and think about this concept.

We will explain how to leverage search on any platform to your advantage in the next chapter of this book. Right now, let's focus on the "crowd-sourced" part of how these sites work. These sites use content created by people just like you. And in deciding which pieces of content to show in their search results, how can they determine which content made by random individuals is better than other content? Just about all these sites use something called "social signals" and "engagement signals" to determine which pieces of content are better than others. The content that has more of these positive signals tends to be propagated up within that particular site, and get exposure to more people. Let's go over how you can make these social and engagement signals work in your favor.

Social signals are things such as Facebook likes, thumbs up

on YouTube, and reviews on product sites. And, of course, the most common social signal of them all is whether people leave a comment or not. Commenting may seem trivial, but most of these crowd-sourced sites view comments as positive social signals. It may seem too simple to be true, but these sites put quite a bit of weight on social signals. And to boost your presence and distribution on those sites, always encourage people to up-vote your content, and comment where that is possible.

Engagement signals are things like the number of subscribers you might have on a YouTube channel or an iTunes podcast. Engagement is also the time people spend listening to a podcast, or watching a YouTube video. The same is true for mobile app stores. If, for example, an app is opened daily by a large percentage of users, and they use that app for a long time each day, the app stores will rank that app higher, giving that app a chance to get more users. Engagement is also something that is relative. These sites typically measure engagement metrics of similar pieces of content. The product or piece of content that has better social and engagement signal typically rises above similar pieces of content with less positive engagement and social signals.

There is one small caveat. Acceleration and speed of acquiring these metrics is key! These large search-based sites don't just measure the totals of your metrics. They measure recent performances of how some pieces of content performed against others in a recent day, week, month, or any period. That means that your content must acquire these positive engagement and social signals at a higher rate than the content of your competitors. But as you rush to increase the rate at which you grow subscribers, likes, and shares, keep in mind that this is a marathon. This isn't a sprint. Focus on the long-term.

You should be planning for how to acquire positive social and engagement signals when you first conceive and plan your social media marketing strategy on any of these large platforms. Planning for how to position your content to have more positive social and engagement signals ahead of time will ensure that acquiring these social and engagement signals will happen naturally from the way your users will interact with your business on that platform.

x. Adding social sharing buttons on your site

Almost every site these days has social media sharing buttons on nearly every page. But are they effective? Which social sharing buttons work best? How many social media sharing buttons should there be on a page? And should they be towards the bottom, or on top of the page? Let's explore these issues.

Number Of Social Sharing Buttons

The optimal number of social sharing buttons for a site or a page is three to eight buttons. More than that creates clutter. And less than that leaves too few options for visitors. Additionally, this is a solid approximate range because you should focus on adding the social sharing buttons of sites on which you are investing in growth. Focusing on just the social sites on which you are making big bets will help you accelerate the growth of your presence there more efficiently.

Which Buttons To Display

The most common social sharing buttons to display on your site are Twitter and Facebook sharing buttons. Those are default social sharing buttons that people almost expect to see.

You also want to have a Google+ social sharing button because Google+ boosts your SEO like no other social network. So if you are doing SEO marketing, which you should be, then make sure to include the Google+ button.

You should also include a social sharing button from one or two social networks that cater to your business niche. After that, throw in a social sharing button for any social sharing network where you or your company may already have a strong presence or wish you had a strong presence. That way you will be able to leverage and grow that presence better.

Should The Buttons Be On Top Of The Page Or The Bottom?

Where you place your social sharing buttons depends on how you want to curate the user behavior on your site.

If the social sharing buttons are on top of the page, everyone will see them. But since the people have not read the entire page, there is less reason for them to share that page. So you may wait until the users get to the bottom of the page. If they get to the bottom of the page, it is likely that they are interested and engaged. And those are the users who tend to share content. So they would be more likely to use the social sharing buttons when they see those buttons at the bottom of the page. You can also place social sharing buttons on both, the top and bottom of the page. That is the most aggressive tactic. Just don't put them on the right hand column of the page because that column typically has much less engagement than the left side of the page.

Effectiveness Of The Buttons

I realize all business owners want people to recommend their business to friends, and hope to achieve a viral effect from the social sharing buttons. Unfortunately, most businesses should not expect too much from the social sharing buttons unless their content is especially made to maximize sharing. People rarely use the social sharing buttons, and when they do, not all of their friends see those updates.

Let's go through an example. Let's say a user uses the Twitter sharing button. An average user has about 200-500 followers on Twitter. Usually over half of those Twitter followers are spam bot followers who are not even human. Additionally, a certain percentage of that person's followers are people who may simply not read tweets. That leaves significantly under 50% of the followers of that Twitter account who may be real people who may actually see that Twitter update. Out of those, there is usually a 1-5% click-through rate on any link in a tweet. That leaves you with roughly under 10 potential visitors to your site from a tweet. And those visitors are not necessarily in your target market. They may be just random Twitter users. Most likely they will just browse your site and leave. As you can see, a tweet is nothing to get too excited about. Approximately the same math can be applied to a Facebook like.

The above is true for most businesses. But there are exceptions. If your business is built to have great content that is known to be viral, then, of course, the above does not apply to your business. Conversely, if there are privacy issues around your business like there may be in health-related or finance-related businesses, expect social sharing to be even less of a factor in your marketing simply because most of your users will want to preserve privacy as much as possible.

Other than the traffic you may get from social recommendations, there is value in social recommendations from their SEO potential. Google has stated (and independent tests have supported) that sites and pages which are shared more will get a slight boost to their SEO from the social sharing.

How To Increase The Rate Of Usage For The Social Sharing Buttons

People will rarely share your site with their friends on social networks because they have your best interest in mind. Some people will have your best interest in mind. But most social sharing is motivated by self-interest. And that is fine because there are plenty of self-motivating things you can possibly encourage.

Many sites, apps or products have features that become better if people use them together with friends. For example, playing games with friends is more fun than playing them alone. Also, inviting friends can help people accomplish a task. Inviting friends to use collaborative features can make people more likely to share your website with friends. As a case study, when I added the feature in my business planning mobile apps for people to write their business plan with friends, that increased the friend-invite rate by about 5% from where it was previously. That wasn't a huge jump, but it was certainly a pleasant and welcome addition, especially since my business apps are not very social in nature. Or consider the game Words With Friends. The entire concept is based around inviting friends. Think of how to incorporate that element in your business.

People will also share your content sharing it makes them seem intelligent, funny, interesting, or original. If the content on your page can allow people to seem that way, that will increase the likelihood of them using the social sharing buttons on your site, and sharing the content on your website.

xi. Viral coefficient to calculate how viral your site truly is

You can calculate how viral a piece of your content will be by calculating something called the viral coefficient. The viral coefficient is invitation rate multiplied by the acceptance rate.

The invitation rate is calculated by taking the number of invites and dividing it by number of people actually accepting the invite. That number is the average number of people you get to come to your site from a single invite.

The acceptance rate is the number of invitee sign-ups per the number of invites. It measures the effectiveness of the invites which are sent.

You can improve both, the invitation rate, and the acceptance rate. To increase the invitation rate, just make that action more appealing to people by leveraging their self-motivating interests, and placing the social sharing buttons on more aggressive places on your website. To increase the acceptance rate, the invites that are sent out must be more appealing. That means increasing the conversion rates of the emails or alerts that go out to invite people.

xii. The net promoter score

The net promoter score itself isn't of as much interest as the concepts and ideas behind this theory. The concept is based on the idea that every business has three types of customers: detractors, neutrals, and promoters.

The detractors give negative reviews about the business. The neutrals don't do anything. And the promoters invite friends, and help you spread the word about your business. Obviously, you want to increase the number of promoters for your business.

To understand what the net promoter score for your business might be, you can survey your customers to see how likely they might be to recommend your company on a scale of one to ten. Then you can average out the results and see where your company ranks. Scores of 8, 9 or 10 are great, and are above average. Scores of 6 or 7 are considered average. And scores below 6 are considered below average. You certainly don't want your business to be in this group. Do what you can to increase the percentage of people who would want to recommend your business to their friends. That will help to increase the number of referrals and shares you get in social media and beyond.

CHAPTER 4: ONLINE MARKETING WITH SEARCH AND SEO

i. SEO (search engine optimization) tutorial

SEO (search engine optimization) is one of the best ways to grow a site because it takes advantage of two key factors: 1) the exact timing of when the potential customer is searching for what you are offering, and 2) they are motivated enough to actually take action to look for what you are offering. That is far better than you randomly reaching out to people in hopes that they would need your product or service.

Because they are already looking for a business like yours, or for what you are offering, it makes website visitors who come to your site via SEO much more likely to convert to actual customers. And that is why SEO traffic is so coveted by business owners.

But SEO has been changing every year and it has gotten to be quite complex. It is also probably the single most competitive form of marketing, with every website in the world competing for a piece of the search traffic that Google can send their way.

But SEO doesn't have to be complex or difficult. In this section of the book, we will go over the basics you need to get you quite far in your effort to get traffic from Google. After that, we will explore how to get benefits of SEO far beyond Google.

Building Links To Your Website

One of the biggest deciding factors of how Google will rank websites in search results are links pointing from other sites to yours. Google's algorithm takes into account the kind of sites that link to your site, how authoritative those sites are, the relevance of the sites linking to your site, and how many links there are in total. For example, if thousands of different sites link to your site, then that must be a sign that many people think your site is worthwhile. On the other hand, if no one links to your site, then the site is probably not that worthwhile yet. And if those thousand sites that link to your site are low quality or spam sites, that also doesn't help you much. You must get links from high quality sites, which are on the same subject matter as your site.

Some of the key factors for determining the benefit of a link to your site is whether the site from which the link is coming from is relevant to your site's topic, and the quality of that site. For example, if cnn.com links to you in a news story, then that is a great link because that link comes from one of the most authoritative news sites in the world. That isn't a commentary on the quality of the actual news reported by CNN. The authority is attributed by Google in terms of search. But if a site like www.spam123.com links to you, then that would not benefit your site at all. In fact, that would be more likely to hurt your site in the eyes of Google, especially if many such sites link to you for some reason.

Some common ways to build links are by guest blogging (somewhat contraversial, and we will address this soon), appearing on podcasts (the podcasters link to you afterwards on their site), answer HARO (sign up haro.com) requests, getting press coverage for your business, or cold-emailing other site owners, asking them to link to you. There is an infinite number of techniques to build links to your site. The strategies we just mentioned are just a few of the possible ways to get links pointing to your site.

Just remember, whatever you do, don't build low-quality links. They are more likely to damage your site than to benefit it. We will cover this in more detail shortly.

On-Page SEO: Create High Quality Pages

While the links pointing to your site help your site seem more authoritative and higher quality to Google, Google also considers the quality of each individual page in deciding whether to rank that page in the top-10 results of Google searches. To have a high quality page, it must cover the topic it is about in depth, and preferably use some rich media like videos (remember the versatility of YouTube?), audio (and the versatility of podcasts), photos, or other embedded rich media. Plus, the page must offer real value to real people who should enjoy the page and get real benefit out of it.

The High-Quality Recipie

Here is my approximate recipe to make a page appear to be high-quality in the eyes of Google. A typical page of content should have at least 300-500 (or more) original words of content that are helpful to whoever was searching for this content. The content should also be written using proper grammar, and without spelling mistakes. And don't just add text to fill space. Make the text helpful and additive to the quality of the page overall. Additionally, add rich media such as photos, videos, powerpoint embeds, or audio.

Target Search Keywords

For every page that you want to rank in Google, you must target some specific terms or keywords that people search for. Choose keywords to rank for that are commonly searched for, yet are not overly competitive (if the term is too competitive, you won't be able to rank in the top-10 of Google's search results).

Use this free tool by Google to research keyword volume and demand:
https://adwords.google.com/ko/KeywordPlanner/Home

We will have much more on keyword research shortly in this book.

Create Content Regularly

Don't just create a few pages and be done with it. Google

prefers sites that create content regularly, and put a lot of care into the quality of their content. Just don't overwhelm yourself with having to create too much content on a regular basis. Keep adding content at a pace at which you are comfortable. This is a long-term strategy so make sure that your content publishing schedule is reasonable.

Focus On The Long Term

Google traffic tends to accumulate slowly over time. It is rare to have great spikes of traffic from Google search traffic. For that reason, it is difficult to rely on Google to be your main source of traffic early when starting your business. It is especially difficult to rely on Google when you first start your business. But once you get a page to rank for a particular term in Google, it usually stays there for a long time, regularly bringing you consistent traffic. But it does take time to get many pages to rank well in Google. So focus on the long term with Google, and it will eventually pay off. Just don't have too many hopes for the short term.

How To Measure Google Traffic

The math to calculate the total traffic that you might get from Google, or any other search platform, is slightly different than the math you might use to calculate traffic from other kinds of sites. In search, once you rank well for a particular search term, you usually rank well for that search term for a period of time, and the traffic you get will accumulate over time. For example, if you get a page to rank for term "abc" and that brings you 1 person each day, but ranks in the top-10 results of Google for one year, that means that the total traffic you will get is 364 people.

If you get a page to rank in the top-10 of Google, it typically stays there for a long time. That is unlike non-search-based platforms because, for example, if you post something on Facebook, a few people may click on the link you post, but that post will disappear from people's Facebook feeds by the next day and you will not get traffic from that post again. So you would need to post updates every day in order to get the same traffic. Plus the quality of the traffic would not be the same because you would be marketing to the same Facebook friends every day you post your update. So new people wouldn't be learning about your business.

Traffic from Google is much better because it drives new people to your site. And those people are seeking out what you are offering instead of you re-posting to your existing audience many times and annoying them. Plus, once you get a page to rank, you can leave it for the most part to just remain there and bring you customers. Although it is a good practice to check back on the pages which drive you traffic to make sure that they still drive you that traffic, and to check whether there is any work or maintenance that needs to be done on those pages to make them even more competitive in search.

ii. Inbound marketing

Inbound marketing is a marketing strategy in which you build content with the aim of having it be highly discoverable, and establish channels on various platforms by which potential new customers discover your business, and eventually engage with your business.

Inbound marketing is one of the gems of the Internet, and online marketing overall. There are a couple of reasons why it is so important and useful to leverage inbound marketing to get traffic. The first reason inbound marketing is so coveted is that it is scalable. The next reason this method of website promotion is so useful is that once an inbound marketing channel has been established, typically it remains in place for quite a while, which means that as a marketer you can move on and focus on establishing more and more inbound channels. The next (and possibly the biggest) reason that inbound marketing is so popular and effective is that typically, the site visitors who come to your site via inbound marketing channels are more likely to convert into clients because they tend to be better leads since they are coming to you, and are likely seeking out whatever services or products you are offering.

Inbound Marketing Channels

The biggest online inbound marketing channel is Google search. If you rank in Google for search terms that are relevant for your business, you will get consistent inbound traffic from the people who are searching for the keywords associated with your business. Google traffic is an obvious first choice, but it isn't correct to just stop there. We must think broader.

There are many channels through which people can find you. They can be YouTube.com, Quora.com, Yelp.com, mobile app stores, or any other (typically search-based) platform where you might have a presence. Try to think about where your potential clients might be, and establish a presence there, which will serve as an inbound channel for your business.

For example, if you have a dentist office, you should have a presence on Yelp because people search for dentists on Yelp because Yelp is a common site for finding local services. People also search for dentists on Google, so if you have a website, people can find your website in Google as well. But let's not stop there. There are dentist-specific sites which can also serve as inbound channels. Now let's get creative. What if you start a dental hygiene class? Can some of the people who attend the class become clients of your dental practice? They definitely can! Your imagination is the limit for establishing the number of inbound marketing channels.

The theme of inbound marketing is to establish the channels where people might discover your business on whichever platforms it may be advantageous to your business to have a presence, and generate inbound inquiries of potential clients for your business.

Keyword Research And Inbound Marketing

Keyword research may be a topic which sounds boring, but it is very important. After all, if people are going to be searching, what keywords will they be searching in order to find your site? And what keywords will bring you the best types of leads for your business?

Let's come back to the example of the dentist. Let's say it is a dentist in Boston. A search phrase like "dentist in Boston" is a great one because the intent behind this search is likely to find a dentist for the person who is searching. And the person searching is likely to live in the Boston area if they are doing a search like that. That means potential revenue for the dentist if the person searching becomes a patient. If you are a dentist in Boston, having your site rank well for a search like "dentist in Boston" is great, but it is not enough. There are many variations of other kinds of searches which can bring you clients. Additionally, people may be searching for something like "my teeth hurt." Now, is that a good search term for you? It is an OK search term. But is it better than "dentist in Boston?" No! The search for "dentist in Boston" is the most direct for what you want. The search term "teeth hurt" suggests that the person needs dental help, but they may not be in the Boston area, and therefore can't become a patient. Nevertheless, there are many different variations of search terms that may bring you good leads.

iii. Full look at SEO keyword research

The process of doing your keyword research to see what keywords might be the most lucrative for your business has to be done carefully and with quite a bit of savvy. There are many parts to it that need to work out well, and if some component is missing, it may damage your entire inbound marketing effort. When you do your keyword research, attention to detail is extremely important. A slight difference in the wording can mean a different type of intent by whoever is searching, making them more or less of a quality lead for your business.

Low Demand Keywords

The first concept to understand is the volume of search demand. You must attempt to rank for keywords that are in high enough demand by people who are searching. It doesn't do you any good to rank for terms that are very rarely searched. Even if you rank in the top-10 of Google search results for low-volume and low-demand keywords, because there are few people searching those keywords, few people will discover your site through those searches.

High Demand Keywords

On the other side of the spectrum of keyword research are the tempting terms and phrases which have gigantic search demand. If, for example, your website is selling shoes, it would be amazing if your site ranked in the top-10 of Google search results for a search like "buy shoes" or simply "shoes" because it would drive a great amount of traffic to your site. And that traffic would be likely to make large purchases, which would be absolutely great for your business.

Level Of Competition For A Keyword

Keywords that are in high demand, and that can drive lots of traffic to your site can be extremely difficult to rank for because the competition to rank for them is immense. Think back to our example of the search for "buy shoes." The first page of Google's search results for that lucrative term is filled with billion dollar companies like Amazon, Zappos, or other large retailers or shoe brands. A small company has absolutely no chance to rank in the top-10 search results for such a term.

You must choose keywords that have a high enough volume of demand, but at the same time these should be keywords for which your site will be able to rank, and where your business will have a chance to be competitive. If you can't get into the first page of results for a particular search term, the entire effort to rank for that term is likely wasted because that page will never get the exposure you were hoping to get with it, and it will never bring you much traffic.

Keyword Research Tool

The Google AdWords keyword research tools is a very nice tool to help you with your keyword research. It allows you to see what kind of search demand there is for any search term. Here is a link to Google's keyword research tool: https://adwords.google.com/ko/KeywordPlanner/Home

Once you find search terms that you feel could drive high quality traffic and leads to your site, that also have a large enough search volume, search that term in Google to see what other sites come up. If the top-10 search results are composed of very authoritative sites owned by large companies, that particular keyword may be too competitive. But if not all 10 of the results are strong sites, you may be able to beat them and get yourself a spot in the top-10.

Finding Your Sweet Spot On Any Search Platform

You must find terms that are not too competitive, that also have high-enough search volume to bring you meaningful amounts of traffic. To do that with Google SEO is admittedly not simple because there is tremendous competition for even the not so lucrative keywords. And that is fine. Google is the biggest search engine, but it is not the only search engine. You can use your keyword research, and try to rank your products on other search engines for the same types of keywords. For example, YouTube is a search engine, the mobile app stores are search engines, local service sites are search engines, Amazon.com is a search engine. Almost every large platform has a strong search component to it where a very large part of content discovery happens through search. What you must do is understand which of these platforms has the traffic that is most relevant to your business, and invest in that search platform to have your listing rank for the keywords which would drive high quality leads to your business.

iv. Case study of SEO beyond Google

When I first started my business Problemio.com (business niche) I had a very difficult time getting Google search traffic because I was competing with some of the biggest business sites in the world for nearly every search term I had hoped to rank for. That led me to look for other inbound and search marketing channels.

Luckily for me, my second choice after Google search was to focus on mobile app platforms. The two biggest mobile app platforms are the App Store from Apple, and the GooglePlay store from Android. They are also large-volume, search-based platforms. Granted, they are far smaller than Google search, but for a small business like mine, any such platform was gigantic in terms of the volume of traffic it could drive to my business.

Even though the app stores are very crowded with apps, the level of competition in the app stores is nowhere nearly as fierce as it is in Google search. Relatively quickly, I was able to create apps that were either dominant, or close to dominant for their main search terms. That led to thousands upon thousands of downloads for my apps. Eventually, my business outgrew the app stores, and I moved on to market via YouTube, podcasting, and other platforms. All these platforms are similar to each other in that they are also search-based platforms. I will cover this journey in much more detail with actionable tips in the chapter with case studies. For now, I just wanted to show an example of how as business owners, we should not rely solely on Google search because there are many more different options out there.

Google search traffic is great if you can get it. But it is also very expensive. It might seem free, but if you recall from an earlier chapter, the cost isn't just the dollar amount required to place the ad. The cost is also the time it takes before you start getting clients from a particular marketing effort. And not even every marketing effort ultimately brings in clients.

In the case of my business, Google search volume never got close to driving the amount of traffic I was able to get from the app stores, YouTube, and other search-based platforms. So keep an open mind for what other possibilities may be available to you. Google search isn't the only game in town.

v. Content marketing strategies

The most common marketing pattern using content marketing is to build a page/video/anything with content on any topic, and then make sure that this page/video/anything is discoverable via search in the platform on which it lives.

Once people discover that piece of content, the pattern is usually to have great content on that page so that the person who finds that page is satisfied. Once they are satisfied, there should be calls to action on that very same page for further actions this user should take to get further involved in your brand.

Do you see the pattern? It works like this: make your content easy to discover --> provide value --> establish trust and credibility --> offer more of your products or services once people trust you.

Let's go over this with a real life example. Since my business helps entrepreneurs, the searches that are of interest to me are ones that entrepreneurs would search. Some examples are "how to pitch your business" or "business pitch template." Let's use the second term for our example. At the moment of writing this book, my YouTube video on this topic is in the top-5 search results in YouTube, and the article I wrote about on this topic ranks in the top-10 search results of Google for that search term. In both, the video and the article, I try my best to explain how to pitch a business, and provide a template with some examples. After there is enough content there where I feel confident that people who were looking for a business pitch template would find that piece of content useful and sufficient, I suggest to the people who are on that page to check out more of my work, and some of my paid products like my books, online business courses, or my paid mobile apps. People who get benefit from my video and web page about this topic will likely want to get more of my content because the content they read or watched was useful to them. So all I have to do is create many such pieces of content through which people can find me work. And there is a near infinite amount of such inbound marketing channels that a business can establish.

The particular search we used as our example is not a very high-volume search. So it does not bring in too many people. But it does bring in people who are in my target market. So most of these leads are quite good. To compensate for the low volume of such search terms, I had to make many pieces of content with each piece of content targeting a different search term each time.

Notice that blogging is a great way to replicate this exact strategy.

vi. Blogging and guest blogging as SEO and content marketing strategies

As mentioned earlier, blogging is just as much an SEO

(Search Engine Optimization) strategy as it is a part of social media. You can post links to your blog posts on social media sites like Twitter or Facebook. And that would allow you to build an audience on those social sites while driving traffic from those sites to yours. Blog posts can also rank in Google for whatever search terms you target with them.

Can Blogging Make Money?

You don't have to view blogging as just an inbound marketing channel. You can also use a blog as your main product, and still make money from a blog in a variety of ways. You can also use your blog to further establish yourself as an expert in your field, and use it as a tool to network and connect with others.

Making money on your blog depends on two factors. The first is how much traffic you are able to drive to your blog. The second factor is how well you are able to monetize that traffic. There is a big difference if you can make $1 per site visitor if you sell something lucrative, or $0.01 on average if you just display advertisements on your blog.

The most common way to make money on your blog is through displaying ads such as Google's AdSense ads. AdSense ads (otherwise known as Google ads) usually make $5.00-10.00 per 1000 page views which means that you can make as little as half a cent on average per page view. That is far too little. Displaying ads is OK, but you need to monetize your site better if it will ultimately become a viable business.

Additional blog monetization options are affiliate sales through sites like CommissionJunction, Amazon, or many other similar sites where you are able to resell products made by other companies, and earn commission. Typically, the revenue you can earn via affiliate sales is much greater than you can generate on AdSense. But it is up to you to get the affiliate sales working effectively which means experimenting with which products you try to sell, and how you try to sell them on your particular site.

Another way blogging can make money is by selling your own products that you make. If you do not have products that you have created, don't worry. There are many digital products that can be easily created. One example of such a digital product are eBooks. You can easily write an eBook on the same topic about which you are already blogging, and sell it right from your blog. Just like you can create digital books, you can create online course and sell those from your site as well. There are many more ways to make money from a blog. But discussing that in detail would be distracting from the main topic of this book, which is marketing. This section is just a brief introduction for how to monetize your blog.

Setting Up Your Blog

To make money from your blog, you obviously need to set up your website and start promoting it.

Setting up a blog is surprisingly simple. You don't need technical skills to set up a blog, or manage it. You can use WordPress. Here is an online tutorial for how to set up your website or a blog quickly, cheaply, and on your own:
http://www.problemio.com/website.html

Blogging To Position You As An Expert In Your Field

Another benefit of blogging is that it can give you exposure as an expert in your subject area. When people discover your blog and read it, if they get value from it, they may want to work with you, buy your products, or hire you for something that they need. Or that person might just become a business contact which is always helpful.

The caveat is, of course, that to position yourself as an expert in your niche, you must write very helpful and insightful blog posts. The extent of your expertise will be judged by the quality of your blog posts and the ideas that you share. If you are going to position yourself as an expert in your domain using your blog, you must make sure that your writing is of very high quality, and provides insight.

Blogging Helps Create An Approachable Brand

Sharing good content on your company's blog (as well as just about every other social media platform) can help your product or service stand out from the rest. A well written blog can take the your company from being seen as a static entity to a brand which is personable, that people can connect to. People will have a reason to follow your blog, and will feel more involved in the growth of the business because they will be updated on all the developments of the business. Plus, having a blog gives people a reason to visit your website on a regular basis.

Blogs, Google Search, Virality, And Social

If your blog posts rank in Google, more users who reach your blog via search traffic will share your site via the social sharing buttons on your site.

If your blog becomes well visited and well ranked, people will automatically want to learn more about your business by browsing around your website, which in turn may result in increased sales and recommendations.

Additionally, if you embed YouTube videos or Podcast audio in your blog posts, your blog visitors will drive up the number of YouTube views or podcast plays, which are positive engagement signals for your YouTube and podcast channels. And that will help the videos and podcasts rank better in YouTube and the podcasting platforms. And if you rank well on those platforms, it will drive even more traffic back to your blog, creating an amazing cycle of goodness where each of these platforms amplifies the others, helping you out-compete your competitors on each of these large platforms.

Do you remember that the acceleration of positive social and engagement signals helps you beat your competitors in large, search-based platforms? A highly-trafficked blog can help you accomplish just that if you use it to drive your YouTube and podcast engagement.

Guest Blogging

Guest blogging is the latest controversial topic in blogging and Google search. In 2008 you would have been called an SEO and blogging genius if you were doing guest blogging. From 2010 to 2012 just about all SEO marketers were doing some sort of guest blogging. In 2013, Google began giving stronger hints that guest-blogging is being overdone, and in early 2014, Matt Cutts who is the chief search engineer of Google's web spam team began to publicly warn against guest-blogging which is done solely for SEO purposes. That means you must tread very lightly when it comes to guest blogging. And if you avoid it entirely, that may just be the most viable strategy. Outside of Google, no one knows what the future of guest blogging will be.

Are There Benefits To Guest Blogging?

For a few years, guest blogging has had three great benefits. It was a good way to get links and traffic from the sites on which you might post. The link you would get would hopefully boost your SEO. Additionally, writing a guest post might help you increase your overall brand exposure.

As you can see, posting guest blog posts in bigger sites has value that goes far beyond SEO. It is simply good marketing because you can get real traffic who may become your customers. The problem with guest blogging is that Google's control of the SEO and blogging ecosystem might make guest-blogging risky, and for that reason you might want to think twice about pursuing guest blogging as a marketing strategy.

Managing Expectations For Your Blog

As site owners, we all want our blogs to grow traffic exponentially. But often, that isn't the case. In fact, the opposite experience is often the case. Blog growth via SEO tends to be incremental, slow, and builds little by little over time. So if you are wondering whether blogging still works, the answer is yes, but likely not to the degree to which you are hoping, and not as fast as you are hoping for it to grow.

As with any business venture, try to understand what it will take to reach your goals for the blog, and the time that it will take to reach those goals. If you go through this process of calculating the potential of your blog, the right way, more often than not, the answer is a bit sobering.

vii. Google penalties

Over the years, with just about all website owners trying to out-market and out-compete one another, you can imagine that some of them tried less than ethical techniques. To remain competitive, the ethical website owners had to also resort to those same less-than-ethical techniques, or have their businesses die due to losing customers to the businesses which were using the not so ethical techniques.

Over time, Google had to crack down on all that. In recent years Google put its foot down by introducing a few very harsh penalties that have killed off thousands of such websites. Let's focus on some of these penalties to make sure that you do not get penalized by Google.

What Happens When Your Site Get Penalized

Google doesn't inform you about getting penalized, and doesn't warn you if you are about to get penalized. The common experience of a website or business owner whose site gets penalized is that they wake up one day, check their analytics to see how many visitors they had in the previous day, and see an absolute cliff in their chart. That is a heartbreaking experience for anyone who has ever put their heart and soul into growing a business. The level of traffic drop it typically very big. And by that point it is too late. It is extremely difficult to recover from Google penalties, and many sites never ultimately recover.

Panda Penalty

Google introduced the Panda penalty in February, 2011. That penalty targeted websites which had thousands of pages with very thin or poor quality content on those pages. Typically such pages were auto-generated by the tens of thousands by these websites in the hopes of having them all rank in Google. And many such sites did rank in Google before the Panda penalty. Then overnight, they were mostly gone from search results. But many innocent sites got destroyed by this penalty as well. It wasn't a perfect update. Most sites which were then penalized have not reported a full recovery even years since the penalty.

In the case studies chapter we will go over an example of one site that got penalized with the Panda penalty.

Penguin Penalty

The Penguin penalty (don't you just love these cute names for harsh penalties which destroyed thousands of businesses and cost tens of thousands of lost jobs?) followed the Panda penalty. The Penguin penalty was released in April 2012.

Sometimes Google tries to distort the extent to which they damage businesses with their penalties. As you continue your research into the Google Panda and Google Penguin penalties, you may sometimes come across them being called Google updates instead of penalties. But make no mistake, if you invest months of effort and thousands upon thousands of dollars on getting Google search traffic, there is nothing cute, soft or pleasant about these penalties. They hit like a freight truck.

Getting back to the topic at hand, the Penguin penalty was designed to punish sites which had been accumulating poor-quality links in order to manipulate search results in their favor. As mentioned earlier, when many links point to a particular site, Google takes that as a positive signal, and ranks that site higher. Many website owners took advantage of that situation by buying many low-quality links from low-quality sites to climb in the search rankings.

Critique Of The Penalties

As you can imagine there is a lot of critique of these penalties in the business and SEO marketing community. Some of the constant points made by business owners are that these penalties come without warning, and with almost no real way to recover from these penalties. Plus, since these were very wide-sweeping algorithm changes in Google search, many innocent sites got thrown under the bus along with the guilty sites. And the worst part of these algorithm changes is that many of the big brands that were the most guilty of the offenses that were punishable by these penalties never got punished. Google has a long history of pardoning sites that belong to big brands and punishing small business owners.

The Bottom Line

Google reserves the right to say that any attempt on the part of website owners to manipulate its search results is a violation of Google's terms of service. This means that anyone doing SEO marketing can potentially be guilty of that accusation.

Additionally, small business owners have no real voice. Yes, they complain. But who hears their complaints? Not too many people. And it isn't to Google's advantage to engage in conversations about these penalties and the effects of those penalties on people's businesses because that paints Google in a negative light, and they just don't want to bring any extra attention to this.

As you can see, SEO is very complex. But SEO remains to be very coveted source of web traffic. There is much more to the SEO industry than can be written in just one chapter, but I tried to offer an objective view of the positives and negatives of Google. How you approach it with your business is up to you.

viii. Cases when you can dominate Google's top-10 search results

When a particular search is very specific, it tends to have less competition. Surprisingly, the quality of the leads that might come in through that search tends to be better because since the search is specific, the person searching knows exactly what they want. And if your site can provide that, it becomes simple to convert that lead into a customer. Let's explore how you can dominate such long-tail, specific searches.

To understand how to dominate the top-10 of Google's search results, think about what kinds of sites usually appear in search results. Search results tend to be full of very established and authoritative sites. Some of the current such sites are YouTube videos, Quora answers, Amazon store listings, URLs to mobile app stores, Yelp listings and other local business listing sites, a Google map with listings, and even PowerPoint presentations from Slideshare.

This means that if there is a particular search term that seems to bring you very high quality leads, it may be worthwhile to invest some resources to get a YouTube video and other types of content made to rank in Google's top-10 for that term. That way your properties can take up multiple slots of Google's top-10 results. The more different types of content you can place on the first page of search results, the higher the chance of landing clients.

ix. How to do paid search marketing (SEM)

Search engine optimization is not the only way to get high quality traffic from Google. In addition to SEO, you can get search traffic via Google SEM which is their paid marketing option. The official name for this is Google Adwords. It is called that because you bid on keywords from which you want to get traffic. If a keyword is popular, and many people bid on it, that drives the price for your ad to appear higher. But if a keyword is not too competitive, the price may not be too high.

Most business owners tend to shy away from "paid" marketing options because there is a psychological barrier to handing over cash to someone else. But as we covered in the chapter on marketing fundamentals, the cost to place the ad is often the smallest cost. The far larger cost is the time that it might take for a marketing campaign to begin working. And with "paid" marketing you don't have to wait at all. When you pay, you get almost immediate traffic. And that enables you to monitor how that traffic behaves, and whether the website visitors whom you paid to bring to your site actually convert into paying customers at a good enough rate to justify continuing to pay for the ad.

How To Take Guessing Out Of SEM

In order to minimize the risk of losing the money that it costs to get website traffic from SEM, you must understand your lifetime customer value (LTV).

The LTV is the cumulative net profit (notice it is profit and not just revenue) that is generated from the lifetime of the relationship of a customer with your business. The concept of lifetime is a tricky one because it is difficult to predict the nature of your product and your overall business years from now. Another issue that makes this figure difficult to calculate is that different kinds of customers behave differently. For example, if someone buys something as a gift, that will be a one time purchase. But if someone buys something for themselves, they may buy it multiple times over the next months and years, depending what that item might actually be.

Most companies spend a lot of time thinking about how to increase their customer lifetime value. But sometimes the customer lifetime value can decrease. It can decrease due to poor economic conditions, increased competition (especially price competition), or the product simply losing popularity.

The reason it is very important to increase your lifetime customer value is that the more money you can earn from each of your customers, the more money you can spend advertising to get each new customer. And that creates a great cycle where you can spend money advertising which directly earns you more money. And since you are paying for the advertising, you don't have to wait for traffic to come later (like you do with SEO).

Some of the ways to increase your company's LTV are to add a subscription model where your customers are billed each month, or at some regular time period. You can also create your product in a way that makes people come back to your company on a regular basis. A perfect example of that is buying a printer, and then having to regularly buy ink cartridges to print. Additionally, things as simple as having great customer service, or a great product can make people come back to do business with you more often.

Once you get a good approximation for your LTV, you will understand what you can spend on marketing to get new customers in a way that is profitable. And if Google's

AdWords (or any other paid marketing platform) will bring you quality leads at a low enough cost, you can escalate that and bring in many customers that way.

Let's think back to the first chapter of this book. Do you remember the concept of the 4 pillars of marketing? It is at work in a near ideal state here. When you can buy traffic from Google, you can target really well. Knowing the LTV and the costs allows you to make sure that this is all done at prices which make sense for your business. And since it makes sense financially, this also means that you can turn up the scale of the traffic you get from advertising this way. And, of course, the last part of the 4-pillars of marketing concept is how well the traffic converts. Here we are operating under the assumption that the traffic converts well since you are able to make profits from that traffic, and you targeted the right people with your keyword selection. In practice, you would need to test conversion. But chances are that conversion would be quite good since that traffic is well targeted.

CHAPTER 5: OTHER ONLINE MARKETING STRATEGIES

i. Ten strategies to get press coverage and publicity for your business

Every business owner craves exposure for their business, and getting press coverage in large publications has potential to give your business very significant exposure, and a chance to get more customers and grow the business. Press coverage is a great way to get the kind of exposure that portrays the business as one of the leaders, and a mover and shaker in its business niche. Let's go over ten different strategies to maximize your business's exposure by getting publicity and press coverage.

One: Get Free Press With HARO

HARO stands for Help A Reporter Out. It is a service where reporters post inquiries about articles they are writing. Those reporters are typically looking for experts in particular areas to give them a quote or a paragraph of insightful information on a certain topic. If you can become a source who provides that quote or paragraph by answering questions from reporters who are searching for authoritative insights, these journalists will credit you as the source in their story, and link back to your site. Most of them will mention your name, your company, and link to your company's website. This has two benefits. In addition to the obvious immediate exposure, your business gets a link pointing to your website from a high quality site, and that helps your long-term SEO efforts.

Two: Create A Press Release And Send It To Hundreds Of Publications Using A Service Like PRWeb

PRWeb is the world's #1 news release service. It provides many free guides and tutorials on how to get press. Even its paid products are very affordable. They are certainly much cheaper than hiring a PR firm. They have free and paid tools to help you create a press release, and then send it out for you to thousands of publications. Naturally, their paid tools and services produce better results. But once again, even their paid tools and services are quite affordable.

Three: Use Your Connections

A great way to get press coverage is to use your connections in the industry. People whom you know may know bloggers, journalists or people working at various publications, and can put you in touch with journalists, and help to get a story about your business published. There are two issues typically preventing people from using this strategy. The first is simple, and it is that many people are simply afraid to ask others for help, and ultimately never ask their connections to help them get connected to anyone who might cover their business. The second issue people face is that not everyone has the types of connections to help them get in front of reporters and influential bloggers. If you do not have those kinds of connections, you can begin building them now, or as soon as possible.

Four: Start Relationships With Journalists And Influential Bloggers

Since you know that you will eventually need to get press coverage for your business, you can begin establishing relationships with bloggers and journalists in your business niche. It is never too early to research the journalists and bloggers who are writing about your industry. Try to create relationships with those journalists online since most of them are probably not all located in your city. If some of them are located in your area, it is a good idea to try networking with them at local industry events, or wherever you can get a hold of them. Face to face connections are much more powerful. And try to connect with them before you actually need the press coverage so that you can build a little bit of a business relationship with them before you have to ask for a favor. They have many business owners approaching them, and asking to get press coverage for their business. So you must try to stand out by having built at least some rapport with them. Just about all journalists and bloggers use Twitter. Follow them on Twitter and interact with them. And when the day comes when you will need press coverage for your business, they will know a little bit about you and will be more likely to consider writing an article about your business.

Five: Hiring A PR Agency

Big or mid-size businesses typically hire a PR agency or an in-house PR team to help them get press coverage. That typically works great for getting press, and is an amazing option for any business that can afford it. The problem is that a typical PR agency typically charges $10,000 per month on retainer. That means you don't just pay for one month. You might sign a retainer deal for at least a few months. That kind of cost typically ensures that this is not a viable option for most small businesses.

Six: Get Press Coverage From (Influential) Blogs

Try to reach out to bloggers in your niche. If you can, offer them something for free (maybe a sample of your product or service) so that they would write a review about your product or service. You can also offer them an opportunity to promote their blog on your YouTube channel or podcast. Many bloggers are much more approachable than large publications. So if you have a hard time getting press from very large sites, try to get press from bloggers in your business niche, or bloggers that blog about business your local area.

Seven: Get Press Coverage By Being A Guest On Radio Shows

Appearing on podcasts and radio shows is also a great way to get press. Just like HARO can help you get press coverage from journalists and bloggers, a site named RadioGuestList.com can help you get press coverage on radio shows and podcasts (Internet radio shows).

RadioGuestList.com sends daily email with information about radio shows and podcasts that are looking for guests. If your business background matches what the podcasters are looking for, you can email them and try to book an appearance.

Note that this can also boost your SEO efforts because very often, podcasts also have a website on which they write about each episode. They can link to your website from their website when they write about the episode on which you were the guest.

Eight: Get Press By Guest Writing

As mentioned in the section about guest blogging, this is becoming a somewhat risky technique due to the dangers of potential future Google penalties. Nevertheless, this is a very viable way to get exposure from bigger sites.

In case bloggers do not want to cover your product or business, you have another way to get exposure from their blogs. You can ask them if they would accept a guest article written by you to place on their blog. In the guest article, you can link to your site. That can help you get clients who may come from those blogs to your site. If you write an article for a blog, that saves the blogger a few hours of work, and gives them content to post on their site. So there is benefit in it for them.

Few suggestions on guest blogging: make sure that the publication on which you are trying to place a guest article is in the same business niche as your business. The content must be relevant to their readers and your audience as well. Additionally, don't over-do it with guest-blogging. A few times a month on different publications should be max. If you are concerned with potential future Google penalties, maybe even fewer guest posts should be the max. When you do write guest blogs, always try to guest-blog on high quality blogs. Don't waste time placing articles in tiny blogs or low quality websites because they will not bring you much traffic, and the links from them will not be valuable for SEO.

Nine: Stand Out And Be Extraordinary

One thing to always think about is how your business can be or seem unique, interesting, unusual, and stand out. When your business stands out, you are more likely to naturally get noticed and get press coverage. Do you remember the section about Seth Godin's concept of the purple cow? Whenever possible, try to leverage that concept to get your business to stand out. It will naturally drive press coverage and increase general interest about your business.

Ten: Be Press!

I am extremely excited to get to this part of the book because I want to point out a nuance which I have not yet mentioned explicitly, but which has been a theme throughout much of the book so far, and will be an even larger part of the book moving forward.

If you have a podcast, a YouTube channel, a blog, an event series, or other media outlets which give you big exposure, whether you realize it or not, you have made a part of your business into a media company, which is press. *You are press!*

That gives you an incredible advantage. Most businesses wait around in hopes of getting press coverage from some big publication. But if you follow my recipe for getting social media exposure, you get the equivalent of great press coverage every day from your own media channels.

It is an absolute paradigm shift in how you can think about

your marketing efforts. Instead of being a small business, hoping for a handout from bigger sites and publications in the form of press coverage, empower yourself by giving your business a strong media presence.

ii. Benefits of establishing a media presence

If you just finished reading the previous section of this book, stop for a second to take a deep breath. Allow for the psychological shift to sink in. You used to try to get press coverage, but now you are press. Now you are media. Feel the power and the potential rushing through your veins. It is real, and it is an incredible advantage. In this section we are going to explore how you can use it to boost your business.

Additional Revenue Streams From Your Media Channels

Now that you have a growing presence on large media channels, companies that do not have that (almost all other companies) want to get exposure on publicity channels like your YouTube or podcast. This means that you can earn extra money right from these marketing channels of yours by accepting sponsors and displaying some form of advertising on those media channels.

For example, if you have a presence on YouTube, you can make money by displaying ads on your YouTube videos. If you have a podcast, you can get a sponsor, and have commercial breaks at the beginning, end, and middle of your show.

Additionally, some businesses would want to be interviewed

on your YouTube channel, or your podcasts. And that means that you can charge them to be a guest on your show.

The ads can be for your own products. If you have your own products that you sell like a book, online course, or anything else, you can promote that right from your YouTube channel or podcast.

People Will Want You To Give Them Press Coverage

If there is anyone out there whose advice you might want, you want to network with, or someone who might have some knowledge about a topic that you are looking to learn about, you can invite them to be a guest on your YouTube channel or your podcast (or both if they need extra convincing).

Chances are that the people you want to have on your show will agree because they will want exposure for their business. Remember, now you are press and now everyone else is hoping you will be kind enough to help them get exposure for their business by covering that business on your media outlets.

During the show in which you interview these guests, you will have 30-60 minutes to pick that person's brain. And guess what, while you are getting to pick their brain, they see you as someone who is doing them a favor because they get the exposure from your media channel. That means you can ask for more favors later! It also means that during the interview you can establish a business relationship which can be a beginning of a mutually beneficial long-term business relationship with a knowledgeable person.

Later in this book we will cover more details of what happens when your business establishes a media presence.

For now, let's continue to explore other online marketing strategies.

iii. Email marketing tutorial

Email marketing is a great way to promote your business. Email tends to have a higher degree of engagement than many other marketing channels. Additionally, people rarely change their email, and once someone gives you their email address, that email will be an effective way to reach them for many years to come.

Email marketing is one of the preferred online marketing techniques by savvy online marketers. It can be a great way to reach out and re-engage your community. It can also be a good way to reach potential new clients who have given you their email, but have not yet become a paying customer.

Growing Your Mailing List On Your Own

Just about every business should be growing the list of their client email addresses. You should have a call to action on your website, or some process for your users or clients to give you their email addresses so that you can send them updates, discounts, or news about what you are doing.

Growing a list of people who want to stay in touch this way can be great because since they opt into getting email from you, they are some of the most engaged users you have. And you want to maintain a relationship with them. This gives you a way to regularly re-engage them, and remind them about your business. That helps to keep your business on the forefront of their minds, and ensures that they do not forget about your busines.

Remember the section of this book about increasing the lifetime customer value? Keeping in touch with your past customers by using email is one of the great strategies to increase your LTV (customer lifetime value) because if you can get customers to re-engage with your business, they will spend more over the long-term.

Buying Email Lists

People often want to skip the hard work of collecting the email addresses of their customers, and wonder whether they should just buy email lists instead of growing their own email list. Buying email lists is tricky because the people on those lists who will get those emails will not know who you are, and will likely not even open the emails. They will likely just flag your marketing email as spam. And that might even have a negative effect because if many people flag your email as spam, the email providers might flag your future email as spam, and send your email right to the spam folder.

The only time it might be reasonable to buy email lists is when the lists are extremely well targeted to match your target audience. Even then, it is questionable how effective that may be because the truth is that it is nearly impossible to tell the quality of the people/leads on the receiving end of those emails until after you have bought the list and emailed the people on that list.

Additionally, if the list is very cheap and affordable, it can be a low-risk option because there may not be too much to lose by buying it. Just don't expect to get great results.

Use A Mass-Emailing Service

Even though you can just send the emails from your own email account or an automated script, you do not want to do that. Your email account will be flagged as spam by the major email providers such as Yahoo, Gmail and Hotmail. If that happens, most of your emails (even to people you know) will very likely end up in the spam folder.

Instead, use a service like MailChimp, ConstantContact, or any other email marketing service. MailChimp in particular allows a list of up to 2,000 to be emailed free. That means there is no risk to give it a try. After you cross their free threshold, they charge a fee per every additional person on your list. But their service helps your emails avoid the spam folder, and they have many pre-designed email templates that will increase engagement of the people who receive your email.

The Title Of The Email Is Extremely Important

People who receive your email will probably be busy and/or skeptical. No one is really that excited about being a part of a mass email list. It is your job to make them excited and curious about what you are sending. The subject line of the email is one of the top things that can convince them to open the email. Make sure the title is catchy, interesting and engaging. Keep the subject line to no more than 50 characters. 30-45 characters is probably the ideal range.

Also, many email providers scan for marketing terms like free, now, discount, or many similar terms that are often used by marketers. Use of excessive explanation marks can also cause an email to end up in the spam folder. You can look up (just search Google) full lists of such terms that email providers use to flag spam. Try to avoid those terms in your subject line, and use them minimally in the body of your email.

The Body Of The Email

Once people open your email, the body of your email should be compelling, and should have a call to action for them to do something that you want them to do. Usually it is to go to some website and perform some action. But it can't be all about that call to action. You also have to make the body of the email compelling and interesting so that people get engaged with it.

Common Email Mistakes

While we have gone over some good-practices for your email marketing efforts, there are some common and simple email marketing mistakes that you can make which can derail your email marketing efforts. Some of the common mistakes that can derail a marketing campaign are naturally exact opposites of the good-practice suggestions outlined above.

For example, bad titles or email body content that is not compelling will just annoy the people who get your email. If the email is not interesting, it is close to spam quality. Also, if the email reads in a way that is disingenuous, that is also a turnoff to readers. Additionally, if you send the email in a way that would increase the chances of having the email end up in the spam folder (these are covered above) rather than the inbox, that is also a mistake. Lastly, don't send the email updates too frequently. Set an expectation for your users or customers so that they know how often they will get email from you. If they opt into whatever email frequency you promise, be consistent with it. And don't send email more frequently than what people opted into.

iv. How to get social, professional, and paid referrals

Business owners often want to know how they can get referrals for their businesses. Let's take a small step back and make a distinction between the kinds of referrals that are possible for a business to get. There are actually two types of referrals, and the second has a twist to it. Let's explore them.

How To Get Social Referrals

Social referrals can come in a few flavors. The most common social referral is the one we come across on social networks. If we see that our friends are using a certain kind of a phone, we also get naturally curious about that phone. And that applies to many different kinds of products. If our friends mention that they actually like this product, that will typically resonate with us.

This situation becomes even more powerful when we are actually seeking out a particular product, or are considering buying a new product. If we are shopping for a phone, we may post a question to our friends on Twitter or Facebook, asking what might be the best phone, or what phone our friends might recommend. Or we might ask our friends in person. And our friends will give us their "social" recommendations.

The challenge with this kind of an approach is that most people do not get asked for product recommendations very often. So this is not something that scales very well, especially not in the beginning when you have a small base of customers who can refer their friends to your business.

So it is trickier to get social referrals than it might seem. Of course, if you can create your product in a way that makes it better when used with a friend, that would make your business naturally sharable. We covered some of the tactics to increase social sharing in the previous chapter. Now let's explore how to get professional referrals.

How To Get Professional Referrals

Professional referrals from other businesses can be a great way to get clients. Let's explore an example of an industry where business referrals from a professional network work amazingly well.

Consider how the medical profession works. If you go to your family doctor who is a general practitioner, that doctor will listen to what might be causing you pain, make a diagnosis, and refer you to a specialist. A specialist is a doctor who specializes in a certain field of medicine. So if you have some skin irritation, your doctor may refer you to a skin specialist. And if you have a foot problem, the doctor may refer you to a foot specialist. Doctors who get referrals from many other doctors are able to get many clients through such professional referrals. Being on the recommendation list of many general practitioners is a gold mine for a doctor who is a specialist because that is how this doctor gets professional referrals.

This isn't only relevant to doctors. This can be relevant to many different kinds of businesses and industries. It is important to always keep an eye out for what kind of a business might be a good referral partner for your business. Try to set up this kind of a professional referral network within your own business niche with as many businesses as possible. Just make sure that these businesses are able to send you high quality leads.

The Difficulty With Creating A Business Referral Network

If your business is new, it is difficult to get professional referrals because the people who might be potentially referring you are probably not too well aware of the quality of your work. And if they recommend you, their own reputation is put on the line. For that reason, most established businesses who can potentially refer many great leads to your business tend to be hesitant to give professional referrals to companies that are relatively unestablished.

The other reason it might be difficult to get a professional network started is that the businesses from whom you want to get referrals, probably already refer clients to other companies just like yours.

But don't worry. There is a way to convince these businesses to send you their referrals. And the way to convince them is to pay them commission or a referral fee. The referral fee can be per lead or per sale. The size and structure of the referral agreement is something that you can work out with the business which will potentially be referring their clients to you. Cash can certainly help to convince people to refer clients to you.

Another way you can get those companies to refer clients to you is by offering them publicity from your YouTube channel, podcast or blog. If you can help to promote them, it will make them much more likely to help you back. And it will help you establish a stronger business relationship with them.

v. Affiliate marketing

You can also be on the receiving end of generating commissions for professional referrals. And that is through affiliate marketing which is the process of earning commissions online by sending leads to other businesses, and earning commissions if those leads perform some action (typically buying something or signing up for something). It is called being an affiliate because you become an affiliate reseller of products or services.

Being an affiliate reseller allows you to do commerce without having to manage inventory, deal with returns, customer service, or shipping. That makes your costs much lower. It also means that your royalty from sales is lower as well because you would earn less of a percentage from the sale since you do less. Nevertheless, affiliate marketing is a great way to sell things online because it avoids so many of the barriers you would have if you literally had to manufacture, ship and manage an inventory of products.

With affiliate marketing, you typically promote products on your own site. When people on your site click on those products and purchase them on your affiliate partner's site, you get a commission for that referral. The commission depends on what that company pays per sale of a product. Each company has a different affiliate offer for affiliate resellers.

Sometimes you may have an affiliate agreement with a particular company. But most of the time, it is good practice to sign up for a large affiliate site which already has contracts with hundreds of companies. You can choose products from those hundreds of companies that you want to resell as their affiliate. Plus, managing all those partner relationships is simple because the affiliate management site which aggregates all those companies takes care of that for you. Some affiliate sites with which you can register are cj.com, amazon.com or many others.

Once you sign up for a site like cj.com or any other affiliate aggregation site, and choose which products you want to resell, they will give you links that you can post on your website to begin selling those products. Keep in mind that you will have to generate quite a bit of traffic to your site in order to generate significant affiliate revenue. Most users do not make purchases or behave the way you want them to.

vi. How to sell products

If your business sells physical products, this section is for you. First, we must make a distinction. There are different strategies to selling a product that you create vs. a product that you get from someone else, and resell it as an affiliate or a partner.

In this section we will cover the nuances of how selling is different when you create the product on your own, or resell another company's product. We will also cover a number of specific tactics for how you can sell your product.

Types Of Products To Sell

Needless to say, there are many very different products that different companies tend to sell. They can be food products, clothing, books, digital products, uniquely designed items, and many other kinds of things. Selling a food item is obviously very different from selling a widget that you make so as you read this section, try to think of marketing strategies that would work for the type of product you are selling.

Options For Selling Your Product In Stores, Offline

If the product is something that you create, you can approach local stores to see whether they would sell that product from their stores. That can be done with food products as well as physical items such as clothing, books, widgets, or anything else.

There are two types of stores you can approach. You can approach independent mom and pop stores, or large chains. Mom and pop stores may not have much shelf space for your products, and may not be able to sell much of it even if they agree to carry your products. You have to sell your product in many such mom and pop stores in order to generate reasonable revenue. And that is a sales and management challenge (or nightmare, depending how you want to look at it).

Large stores, on the other hand, tend to have many options for what they can sell in their stores because many small business owners approach them on a regular basis, trying to get those large chains to sell the products created by those small businesses. Plus, they know that many small business owners are desperate to sell in their stores. That gives the big chains great negotiating power, which means that they typically offer very bad deals to new companies. Plus, the application process for getting a product into their store is quite lengthy and often expensive in a number of ways.

If you do not create your own product, it is more difficult to sell that product in stores because the original manufacturer of those products can contact the retailers to sell their items directly.

There is an option that can work for all kinds of products, and that option is to sell the products at flea markets, or from carts, or the street. I realize that this option does not seem glorious, but it can result in revenue, and most importantly, when you try to sell that way, you get to see how people react to your product. Plus, you get to hear some of their feedback about the product that you are trying to sell. Hearing that feedback and engaging in conversation with potential customers is invaluable because if you get direct feedback (which you would not get if you sold your items only from stores) you can then take that feedback and use it to improve your product until it is something that customers absolutely love.

Once you get to a point where spending a day selling from a cart or a flea market becomes profitable, you can stop selling there, and simply hire another person to sell there. Once that situation begins to be profitable, you can replicate it by creating multiple similar locations from which people whom you hire sell your products.

Selling Your Product Online

On the web, you have many options for where and how to sell your product. You can sell from your own website, or sell your product from numerous other websites such as Amazon.com Shopping.com Etsy.com or a number of other ecommerce sites depending on which sites make sense for the type of product you are trying to sell. Keep in mind that those sites all use search as a big part of product discovery. So use the SEO skills you picked up earlier in the book to get ahead on the ecommerce sites.

To sell from your own site, you can easily set up a WordPress site and begin selling from it in as little as one or few days. The challenge with that approach is that you will need to bring lots of traffic into your site.

What you want to do is to diversify how you sell online by selling through your own site, and selling your products on the big sites. These two strategies don't have to be mutually exclusive. If you make your own products, you can sell them from Amazon, Etsy, Fab.com, eBAY and many similar sites which allow you to sell items you create. And if the item that you sell is created by a different company, you may have a more limited choice of platforms from which you can sell that product.

SEO Tips For Selling Products

Consider the kinds of content that can show up in Google's search results. Sometimes there are small and independent websites. Sometimes there are Amazon listings. Sometimes there are YouTube videos with product reviews. And at other times there may be Quora questions. What you can do is have a presence on all of these platforms so that your product can have a chance to show up in multiple listings of the top-10 Google search results.

vii. Mobile app marketing

If you are trying to promote a mobile app, the advice in this section is what I personally used to generate hundreds of thousands of downloads for my Problemio.com apps. This should work phenomenally for you as well.

App Store Search Optimization (ASO)

The app stores are the number one driver of app downloads for the vast majority of apps. There are three things you need to do to optimize your app store listing to get the largest number of downloads possible.

First, focus on app store SEO (search engine optimization). In the app stores, SEO is called ASO (app store optimization). Many things we covered in the chapter on SEO should help you when you do your ASO. You must understand what keywords to try to rank for in the app stores, the amount of competition for each keyword, and the amount of demand for the keywords.

Once you understand what keywords you want your app to rank for, create a professional app logo, beautiful screenshots, and write an amazing description and title that are rich with the keywords you are targeting, but also very appealing to people. After all, the search engine is a machine. But the people who will be downloading the app are real people. You must appeal to people's senses and get them excited about your app.

Lastly, once people download your app, make sure the app is engaging. Work on increasing the amount of time people spend on your app, and the number of times people open the app. Those are engagement signals which are ranking factors in the app stores. Remember the section about using positive engagement signals to outrank your competition in large-volume, search-based platforms? This is a great example of such an instance.

If you do the above items well, you should be getting hundreds of downloads per day from the app store. If you are not, then think again about your keywords, and about how well you have implemented the above suggestions. Can they be improved?

Lastly, make sure your app gets good reviews. The reviews are a big part of your app store listing. First and foremost, your app must satisfy your users. Otherwise, everything else will be that much more difficult.

Pro tip: do you remember when we covered how flexible YouTube can be as a platform? You can add your YouTube videos to your mobile app. The videos will increase the time people spend on your app, and that will help you rank better in the app stores!

Get Press Coverage For Your App

Every app developer wants to get press coverage, but less than 1% of new apps are covered by major tech or general news publications. Even apps that do get coverage, either do that through hiring a PR agency (which costs thousands of dollars per month), have great connections, or just have incredibly amazing apps that are truly above the others.

To get press coverage and publicity for an app without hiring a PR agency, being very good is not enough. The app and its story have to be amazing because there are already thousands of good apps out there. The bar of quality to get publicity is quite high.

We covered how to get press coverage in an earlier section. But with apps, there is twist. The app world has quite a bit of hype around it. And you must leverage that hype because if you have an app, that is actually a little bit of a purple cow right in itself. It makes you unique and interesting.

Here is a brief overview of some techniques that work well to get press coverage for mobile apps. First, go to iTunes and search for podcasts in your business niche. Email the hosts of those podcasts to see whether they would have you on their podcast as a guest. Someone who is promoting an app is typically an interesting guest for a podcast audience because many of them often have an interest technology. You will not only leverage the exposure of the podcasts (talking about your business for 30 minutes), but you will usually also get a link to your site, which will be good for your SEO.

The next thing you want to do for publicity is to join HARO. HARO stands for help a reporter out. When reporters need sources for stories they are working on, they email HARO. If you answer HARO inquiries, you can get exposure from all sorts of publications. Your humble author has been able to get exposure for various businesses via HARO in large publications like Website Magazine, Mashable, CBSNews and many other large publications that would be nearly impossible to get mentioned in if it wasn't for HARO. I know firsthand that HARO can work. Again, think of the SEO value of the links you would get from sites as authoritative as the ones I just mentioned.

Social Sharing From Social Networks

Don't view social media marketing for your app as just posting updates to Twitter or Facebook. Think back to our broad social media marketing strategy which gives your business a very strong media component. If you are able to establish a large presence on social networks that way, you can drive many people to your app from social media every day.

Social Sharing From Inside The App

As your users use your app, there will inevitably be some things that they can do on your app with friends or people they know. That can be playing a game together, sharing content, or as the case in my business plan apps, writing a business plan, marketing plan or a fundraising plan together with their business partners.

Whatever features you create on your app, think about whether people would want to use those features with people they know. If so, allow users to invite their friends to download the app and begin using those features together. That will give your app a lift in downloads from your existing users bringing you new users.

Promotion From Your Website

Your website should also be generating downloads for your app. You can drive people to your website via Google SEO, guest blogging, social media, answering questions on Quora, posting on Reddit or participating on other sites within your niche. Then from your site, you can have a call to action (a big button or a highly visible link) for people to get your mobile app.

You can do a few things on your website. Most mobile app sites are just glorified landing pages that are made for one thing only: to get you to download the app. The challenge with that approach is that there isn't a lot of content on those sites to promote other than the app itself, which gives you few promotional angles.

To give you more flexibility in promoting your site, you can maintain a blog on your site. On the blog you can create an unlimited amount of content (inbound marketing!), which you can then promote via SEO and your social media marketing channels. By promoting that content, you will then be able to drive traffic to all those pages, and encourage people to download your app.

There are two options for your blog. You can maintain a blog on your site, or you can have an entirely different site for your blog like I do with Glowingstart.com. The advantage of having a different site is that you can try different promotional strategies on two different sites, and compare results. Additionally, the topic of your blog will only loosely need to match the topic of your app, which will give you more creative freedom to advertise. And, of course, the advantage of having a single site on which you promote everything is that you can focus on it that much more.

Other Apps And Websites

This is one of my least favorite approaches, but it can work. Simply find partners who are willing to cross-promote with you. You can drive people to their websites or apps, and they can drive people to your app. The key is to make sure that you would get as much exposure as you are giving to your partners. Remember, whenever you are sending one of your users out of your app, and to your partner's app, you are killing engagement of your app, which is damaging to your app store optimization (ASO). For that reason, this is one of my less favorite approaches. So think twice about whether you want to do this.

In practice, it is nearly impossible to drive as much traffic to the app owned by the other business as they drive to yours. Someone always has the short end of the stick just because different apps have different levels of distribution and user activity. So you may end up with the raw end of the deal.

Paying For Advertising

You can certainly get downloads by paying for ads on mobile apps and websites. This can be viable, but only once you have established and proven your business model, and understand your lifetime customer value.

Email Marketing

As part of maintaining a blog, or via features inside your app, you can collect the email addresses of your users. That will enable you to reach those people whenever anything noteworthy happens that you want to announce and promote.

For example, if you have an app update or a new app release, you can send a message to your email list and drive them to your new offering, and ask them to recommend the app to their friends. In addition, you can always make additional money from your email list by notifying them of new things you are selling, or any other kinds of discounts or offers moving forward.

Speak And Present At Events

There are many benefits to speaking at events. Of course, the obvious benefit is that the audience may download your app. Yet, that is only a minor benefit compared to the full potential of speaking engagements.

If there are reporters in the room, they may include your app in an upcoming article or story. If there are bloggers in the room they may blog about your app. Those types of things may result in far more downloads than you can generate from the actual act of speaking at the event. Plus, they have lasting SEO benefits.

Additionally, the conversation of the evening will be focused on your business and your app, which can result in plenty of feedback about your product, further introductions and beginnings of interesting business relationships.

Create A YouTube Channel And/Or A Podcast

Having a YouTube channel or a podcast may not

immediately make sense, but it actually makes amazing sense for a number of reasons.

First, YouTube is the second largest search engine in the English-speaking world. Many potential new users can discover your app there, and you can drive many of those potential users from YouTube to your app.

The next best thing about YouTube is that its videos can be re-purposed in many ways. If you want, you can place your YouTube channel inside your app. Having videos people can watch inside your app will help you increase time people spend on the app. And that is a great engagement signal for your app to have.

You can also embed the same videos on your website, which will increase the time people spend on your website. And that may possibly result in higher ranking of some of your website's pages.

Additionally, your YouTube videos may show up in Google search if your actual website doesn't. Recall that Google sometimes displays YouTube videos in its search results.

And if all that wasn't enough, for many types of content, YouTube videos are often more likely to be shared because people like watching videos over reading text. It is often easier to consume video content rather than reading text. Plus, if all else fails, you can make money with YouTube videos by placing AdSense ads on them. YouTube is possibly the most versatile platform. And your videos can be used for many purposes.

Keep Your App Freemium

Have you noticed that most apps in the app stores are free?

That isn't because app developers don't want to make money. It is because app stores make it much easier to promote free apps. And by virtue of that, paid apps never end up ranking well in app store search, and most consumers never see most paid apps because due to the internal nuances of how the app stores work, paid apps are much more difficult to discover.

The common approach is to make your app free to download, which would help to make your app easier market and promote. And once you are competitive in search, and are getting downloads, hopefully you will be able to figure out how to make money inside the app by selling something or in the worst case displaying ads. Most of the top earning apps use the freemium model.

Google Search (SEO) For Your App URL

I saved this tricky one for last. Your app has a Web URL on iTines and GooglePlay. That isn't the same thing as the URL of your website. And you can boost the SEO of the URL of your app by pointing links to it.

While you cannot really track how many people click on, or see the URL of your app, the URL for the app store listing does show up in various Google searches. And you can do SEO for that URL in order to get it ranking well. In fact, quite often the web URL of your app will outrank your website because it is on a very strong domain (Apple's or GooglePlay's). So try to see what keywords your app URL ranks for, and try to point some links to it in order to get it to rank well in search.

viii. Marketing a local business or a

local service

A local service or a local business is a type of business that operates within a certain local radius. Some examples include home repair, cleaning services, doctors, dentists, restaurants, even lawyers, and any other businesses which are only able to serve people within a particular area.

If the type of business you have is categorized as a local service, many of the marketing efforts need to be made locally, or have a local focus.

There are many strengths of such businesses. Couple of those strengths are that they tend to be very useful and proven types of businesses. And when people need those types of services, they tend to search for someone who can provide the services. That is key. Your customers will be searching for you, and you must leverage that by making sure that they find you on whatever platform they may be searching.

If your mind is beginning to think something like "oh, we are just going to use our SEO techniques to dominate on different large platforms where our potential customers may be searching" then I am proud of you. This is exactly what you should do, and you have all the tools and knowledge to beat your competition on those platforms.

Leveraging Search

We have to craft a marketing strategy to ensure that people local to your business find you (and not your competitors) when they search for your type of service. Before the Internet, businesses used to put ads on something like the Yellowpages. This was an extremely thick phone book with listings of all kinds of local services in your city, ranging from plumbers to flower shops to home repair businesses. And people searching for services would find the services they needed by browsing the services listed in the Yellowpages.

The Internet largely replaced the Yellowpages, but the mental pattern of searching remains very similar. We just have to make sure that people find your business when they search on different websites which have replaced the Yellowpages.

The first step is to have your own website. It is easy to create a Wordpress site in a day or two. Having your own website will enable you to rank in Google for searches like "service_type in city_name_you_are_in" and similar searches. The website will also serve as an extra source of information about your business when people want to learn more about your services once they are engaged in the sales process. With your website, you have to focus on ranking in the top-10 of Google for searches that are relevant to your business, and that would bring you high quality leads. Ranking your website for local service is usually pretty competitive. It isn't simple, but in most cases it is doable. The viability of ranking in the top-10 of Google search results for the keywords that are relevant for your business depends on how many other similar services are going to be competing with you in your local area, and how much time and effort you will invest into getting your site to rank in search results.

Additionally, when you create your website, you need to install analytics software to see how many people are visiting your site, and from what sources they are coming to your website. If you have your own website, you can use the free analytics tool from Google called Google Analytics which is an industry standard and very easy to set up.

Leveraging Large Local Service Sites

Once you have a website, you can list it along with your other business information on local service sites such as yelp.com redbeacon.com angieslist.com and many other similar sites, including local service websites that are specific to your industry. Industry-specific sites may be ones which list only dentists, only restaurants, or only doctors. You would have to look up which such sites have a strong presence in your area of business. Different such sites are popular in different parts of the world. The simplest way to understand which such sites might be good for your business is to simply do a Google search for some of the searches that would be relevant to your business. Browse the first 100 results (just to be thorough) and note any site on which you can list your business.

Leveraging GoogleMaps In Search

You also need to add your business to something called GooglePlaces (now renamed to Places For Business). Adding your business listing to Google's Places For Business will enable your business to come up inside a Google map when there are maps with local businesses displayed in Google's search results. If you have ever wondered how businesses get onto that map, it is by adding their information in Google's Places For Business.

Being listed in search results this way is great because these maps usually appear very high on the first page of search results. And they often crowd out other sites. That means that these listings tend to have very high click-through rates.

Basic Social Media Presence

Basic social media presence is not as important as leveraging inbound marketing channels and search, but you should still have a basic social media presence. Create Facebook and Twitter pages for your business, and cross-promote all your web properties (your website, your local service listings, and your other social media accounts). You can link to your website from all your social media profiles, and your yelp.com profile, and other sites on which you post your business profile. That should give you a small SEO boost, and should help your website rank in google searches.

Additionally, if you have the resources to do it, consider doing more advanced social media marketing like we covered in our social media marketing chapter, where you create a very strong media component for your business, and establish yourself as a thought leader and an authority in your business niche.

Paid Marketing Options

The options above don't require paying for them. This option is going to cost you actual cash, but it may be worth the money. At least you should experiment with it at some point to determine whether you can make it work for you.

You can advertise your business by bidding on relevant keywords on yelp.com and GoogleAdwords. That will get your business listing to appear in their promoted listings, next to what they call "organic" search results. It will give you extra visibility when people are searching for the type of service you offer.

Note About Your Listings

Make sure that on Yelp and everywhere else where you list your business, you have good reviews and a good reputation because that helps you rank well and stand out. Additionally, always have a nice logo, nice title and a full and compelling description.

ix. What is network marketing? Is network marketing a scam?

Be careful when people promise you get rich schemes that are easy. If you notice, in this book, the single secret to marketing success I offer is hard work. That can be found in chapter one with the rest of the fundamentals.

Let's define network marketing. Network marketing involves two things. First, you market and promote some products. That is perfectly fine. We all do that as marketers. But the second thing you do is recruit a network of people to also sell those things. And you get a small commission on whatever they sell. But that isn't it. The people you recruit, should also recruit. And that network chain never ends, with you earning some commission from every sale by every recruit down the chain.

For one reason or another, network marketing schemes tend to be marketed by showing you glimpses of a lavish lifestyle that you too can have if you get started.

This isn't necessarily a scam, but it is deceiving because no one tells you just how hard you will have to work in order to pull this off. And that is something you have to keep in mind. To make this work for you, you will need to make this your life, and spend all your time selling, recruiting other people to work under you, and making sure they are working as efficiently as possible. Whatever you do, just don't fall for the hype of this marketing technique and think that the riches will just come. That is where people go wrong. Only explore this option if you are willing to work extremely hard for a long period of time.

x. Event marketing: how to promote events

At first glance, event marketing might seem to be an obscure topic that few businesses might find useful. But that would be a big mistake.

Many different types of businesses should organize, host and run events or workshops as a part of their marketing strategy even if their core business has little to do with putting on events. The events can be a way to attract new clients, and promote the business. Being at the center of an event series is also another way to establish your business as an authority in its niche. Additionally, events are something that can be done on a regular basis. Once your events become successful, you can keep doing them on a regular basis to attract new leads for your business. And if all that wasn't enough, events can also be an additional revenue source for your business because once the events become popular, you can charge attendees directly for attending. Let's cover some common issues involved in organizing a successful event series.

Scheduling The Event

Marketing and promotion of the event starts with the scheduling of the event. If possible, try not to schedule the event at a time when it will be competing with other, similar events or some other very large events. Also, make sure you schedule the event far enough ahead of time to give yourself time to market the event and allow people to work it into their schedules.

How To Title And Describe The Event

The first thing people will see when they learn about the event is the title of the event. The title must sound amazing. Try to make it exciting and inviting. If the title gets people interested, they will try to learn more about the event, and take further steps to learn more about it. One of those further steps would be to read the event description.

The event description must also be well written and compelling. But both the title and the description must also be true. Don't over-exaggerate or over-promise how great your event will be. Try to make the event itself as great as the description. If the event itself is not as good as promised, people will be disappointed.

The purpose of having a great title and description is two-fold. The first benefit is that it helps you maximize the conversion rate of people who see the event to those who sign up to attend. The second benefit is that when you try to promote the event, a great title can catch the attention of journalists and bloggers who cover events. We will go over an example of such a case in the next chapter when we take a look at some case studies for different businesses.

Promoting The Event Online

The Internet is a great place to promote events. In addition to promoting the event on your own website, there are many event sites, blogs, and various community sites which have large audiences that you can leverage to drive potential attendees to your event listing. You can advertise your event on all of them. It is usually free to list your event on most such sites.

If you really want to get the most out of the sites on which you can promote your event, there are two ways to do that. The first is to simply pay a little extra to have your event featured. The second is that you can make your event seem so amazing from its title and description that it can cause those same websites to naturally feature your event because they want the best events to be prominent on their sites.

How To Get The Most Out Of Social Referrals

The best time to ask people to share your event is right after they themselves sign up. After people sign up, they are excited about your event. Once they sign up, offer them ways to share the event with their friends.

Be Consistent

Most events are not an immediate hit. You must constantly refine and improve your marketing efforts, and the quality of your events. Just keep your expectations realistic and keep trying. Consistency will also give you a chance to experiment with your marketing or event themes. Over time, you will learn how to put on successful events. Just don't quit if at first it doesn't work. Later in this book, there will be a case study of my own successful event series which didn't work in the beginning, and required consistency and persistence.

Event Marketing With SEO

You want to make sure that your website and individual

event pages rank for search terms like "event_type in your_city_name". For example, if the event is a group hike in San Francisco, when people search Google for "San Francisco group hiking" your events should easily come up in search.

After The Event

When people sign up, they usually leave their email addresses or like your Facebook page. Try to collect the contact information of people who sign up for your events. If your events provide a great experience, many people would welcome reminders of future events. Keep in touch with them, and update them about upcoming events.

xi. What is growth hacking

Growth hacking is a relatively new term in marketing. It is frequently used in start-up companies because a new company may create a theoretical marketing plan, but ultimately does not know which marketing strategies will work until those strategies are executed and the results are measured in the real world.

Growth hacking is the process of trying different marketing strategies, and seeing their effectiveness. In most cases, things won't work as well as hoped. But in some cases, they will work very well. And growth hacking is the process of trying each potential marketing tactic, seeing which of them will work, and finding the few growth strategies that prove to be extremely effective.

In the next chapter we will go over some case studies which show examples of growth hacking at different kinds of companies.

CHAPTER 6: CASE STUDIES OF GROWING DIFFERENT BUSINESSES

i. Problemio.com case study

Problemio.com is a company with a mission statement which reads as follows: "Problemio exists to help and support entrepreneurs during the process of starting, planning and growing their businesses in order in increase the chances of success."

In 2013, through its various media channels, Problemio reached over 500,000 people, and is projected to reach well over 1,000,000 people in 2014. The projections are based on the acceleration of growth in Q3 and Q4 of 2013.

Problemio was started by your humble author during late 2011 as a half-baked, experimental website that was supposed to help entrepreneurs crowdsource business ideas, and then crowdfund those business ideas to help them become viable businesses. That business idea was a complete failure because people didn't want to discuss their business ideas with each other and preferred privacy. Additionally, my initial marketing efforts were not effective, and I was not able to get any significant traffic to the site.

For a period of time I quit Problemio because it was a failed idea, and began to teach myself how to make mobile apps. In April 2012 I released my first Android app. Since I didn't have any unique mobile app ideas, I rebuilt most of the features of the original Problemio.com website in a mobile app version.

Mobile users didn't want to use the features of the app as I conceived of those features just like web users didn't want to use them. But there was something unique about the mobile app experience. From the very first few weeks of the app being live, I was able to generate 50-100 downloads of the app per day by having people simply find the app in GooglePlay's app store. And monitoring how those initial users used my app allowed me to understand what my users needed, and to rapidly update the app with features that these users needed.

Aha Moment One

The product was essentially the same as it was as a website, but with one caveat. I was able to get steady traffic from the app store because app store SEO (ASO) is not nearly as crowded or competitive as Google SEO.

There was one interesting feature that I added to the app. I allowed my app users to ask me any business question they wanted, for absolutely free. That gave me the opportunity to talk to hundreds of people, and to get to know every possible need that the users of my apps had. After talking to so many people, I got to know the needs of my app users better than they themselves knew their needs because I had a holistic view of their situations, and understood what was waiting for them at each step of growing their businesses.

That allowed me to add features to the app that I knew my users would love. Once I started doing that, the app grew rather quickly on Android because I kept being updating it with things that I learned previous users needed or wanted. There were many "one step forward, two steps back" moments, but overall, the app grew quite nicely. The initial distribution from the app stores was the lifeline this business needed in order to improve its product.

In just 2-3 months, the initial app became the top-rated business app on Android by user reviews, and I realized that I may be on to something so I started to teach myself how to make the iPhone version of the same app. I released the first version of the iPhone app during late summer 2013, which doubled downloads because now I had a product on two large-volume, search-based platforms: GooglePlay and the Apple App Store.

One problem with apps is that they can typically only rank well for a few high-volume search terms. So while my app was dominant for a term like "business plan" in app store searches, I had no presence for terms like "business ideas" or "marketing" or other similar high-volume business keywords.

That prompted me to make additional apps in order to rank for more keywords. My first app evolved into a 4-app course covering business ideas, business planning, marketing and raising money. See how I leveraged the keywords along with meeting people's needs? Those apps are not just about keywords. These are truly the issues that entrepreneurs face most often.

The 4-app course came out on iOS (iPhone and iPad) and Android during Spring of 2013. That was another inflection point of growth for the company, with the apps generating over 1000 downloads every day ever since then. Later that Spring I added a "plan with a friend" feature where users could invite friends to plan their business together, right on their mobile devices. Do you remember that tip from earlier chapters about maximizing your social referrals by letting people do things on your product together? This increased downloads by a further 2-5% depending on the app.

Another inflection point of growth for the apps happened during the middle of the Summer of 2013. I had a professional designer redesign the logos for my apps. I didn't think that this was going to have a huge impact, but it did. To my own disbelief, that single change resulted in about a 15% download increase! But at that point, I was already maximizing the downloads I could get out of app stores search, and needed explore other large-volume platforms.

Even by that time, I was not able to generate a significant amount of SEO traffic from Google, partly as a result of being in a very competitive niche. So the next biggest platform I decided to conquer was YouTube. YouTube seemed like a great choice because I could make money directly from YouTube while also promoting my mobile apps on YouTube, and generate revenue that way. Plus, YouTube offered a great way for me to make a personal connection with thousands of entrepreneurs (remember the value of making a personal connection?) by allowing them to see me on video rather than just read things I wrote.

While YouTube was a natural choice for many reasons, it is quite difficult to establish a strong presence on YouTube, and to get large exposure on that platform. I had to choose a strategy very carefully.

For reference, here is the URL for the YouTube channel: http://www.youtube.com/user/Okudjavavich

Here is the marketing strategy I chose for the YouTube channel. I would have to make hundreds of videos, with each video targeting a long-tail search term. That would enable me to compete in search since going after competitive search terms was not going to be realistic for me to compete in just because I would have to compete against many established YouTube channels and videos. I had to start small.

I would also need to grow the number of subscribers on my YouTube channel to gain authority in YouTube's search algorithm. From ranking well on YouTube, many of my videos would also come up in Google searches (SEO) for those search terms, and that is how I would get most of the views for my channel. This strategy allowed my to have a chance to get exposure on two gigantic platforms: Google and YouTube.

That strategy took 6 months to begin fully working, and is resulting in increased revenue, both from the ads that are displayed directly on the videos, and the mobile apps (and now books and online courses) which I try to sell on the YouTube channel as well. At the time of writing this book, the YouTube channel gets between 500-1000 daily views, and growing.

The success of the YouTube channel signaled that it was a good bet to invest in similar platforms, and in January 2014 I launched my podcast on iTunes and Stitcher Radio. The podcast is just audio from my YouTube videos so it doesn't take much extra time to produce, but gives my business exposure on two additional large-scale, search-based platforms which are iTunes and Stitcher. Additionally, in January and February 2014 I published two books (this book being one of them). The other book focuses on going from a business idea and business planning, to raising money and starting a business. That gives my business extra exposure on Amazon.com and Fiverr where I am selling the books.

In addition to the above strategies, I also write regularly for two online publications about topics that are relevant for my business. Each of the articles I write is seen by 3,000-10,000 readers. That drives additional traffic to my business. Over time, I have also been a guest on over 50 different podcasts.

From this case study, I hope you see how, one by one, I went through each large-scale, search-based platform and used each of them to cross-promote all the others. That helped me beat my competition in each of these platforms, and move on to conquering the next platform. I hope you can take away some of the strategies I outlined here, and use these strategies to promote your business.

ii. HakaLabs.co case study

HakaLabs is a company that helps technology companies hire some of the best and most talented software engineers.

The company's challenge was to attract a great volume of

software engineers so that technology companies would want to work with HakaLabs to get a chance to hire some of those top engineers. But how does a company attract a large number of software engineers? That was the challenge!

Part of the challenge was that it was difficult to immediately begin to leverage high-volume, search-based platforms because the types of searches that engineers usually make are for technology tutorials, and the intent behind those kind of searches does not translate well to getting those engineers to be interested in jobs at tech companies. So at first, HakaLabs took a different approach, and that was to leverage events (offline marketing!) to put themselves in the middle of the software engineering community.

The company was based in New York, which is the second biggest hub for software engineers in United States. The company chose to be very active offline by hosting tech events and having a strong presence at tech events hosted by other companies. Over time, they got to know many of the local CTO's (Chief Technology Officers), and many of the best software developers. They got to make personal connections with many of them by being able to talk to them at the events.

Additionally, HakaLabs always recorded the tech events, and used the video in a number of ways. First, they posted those videos on their YouTube channels. Second, they took the audio from the videos, and made them into a podcast. Third, they created blog posts on their website where they embedded the videos and podcast audio.

That gave HakaLabs a chance to market themselves on YouTube, Google SEO, and iTunes/Stitcher. Since the events they covered had some of the top tech engineering talent presenting, the videos were quite good, and got lots of natural social sharing on social networks. That allowed the company to build a brand that was recognized for providing some of the top engineering content.

They built their audience in two very distinct ways. They had a strong offline component with the events, and they were able to leverage that to help them to become a technology media company. With those two initiatives, they were able to grow quite nicely, and gain recognition among software engineers which made them attractive for technology companies to hire as recruiting consultants.

Additionally, HakaLabs invested in growing an email list. Every week they send out a newsletter with some of the top tech content of the week to their email list. That helps them keep in touch with some of their users, and update them when there is any new development or initiative in the company. If HakaLabs ever releases a product, or launches anything, you can be sure the people on their email list are going to be notified about it, and will be likely to respond positively.

iii. Comehike.com case study

Comehike.com was one of my earliest initiatives which did well. And through my efforts of growing that business, I learned an incredible amount from my mistakes, and will share some of what I learned here.

Comehike was originally conceived of as a website which would be a community site for people who like to hike. The main thing people did on that site was organize hikes, and have other hikers join their hikes. In hindsight, I don't think this is a great business idea. But nonetheless, that is the idea I tried.

As a young entrepreneur I had made a few mistakes during the planning phase of the project. One of the biggest mistakes was a miscalculation of the effectiveness of my monetization strategy, which initially was to make money with ads. Another mistake I made was to underestimate just how difficult it is to create and foster a community on a website. Additionally, I grossly underestimated the need for great design for such a site. To this day, comehike.com has very poor design.

When I first created the website, the website had almost no visitors. Immediately I started working on Google SEO, and reaching out to existing hiking groups to see whether they would want to use my website to help them organize their hiking groups. While the SEO efforts started to ever so slightly drive traffic to the site, because the site was new, unproven, and had "not-so-great" design, people didn't trust it enough to start organizing their hiking groups on the site, or to even spend a lot of time exploring the site.

Growing and monetizing this business was much more difficult than I originally anticipated, and I had to find a way to pull this company up by the bootstraps. I started to organize and lead hikes to make the site appear like many (or at least some) people were using it, and also to get people who have attended past hikes to have a reason to come back to the site on a regular basis since there would be new hikes multiple times a week.

The problem was that no one was really attending my hikes. I had too-few visitors to my website, and otherwise, no one knew about the hikes.

In hindsight, a good marketing tactic would have been to

create an account on meetup.com (a leading group activity site with many hiking groups on it) and leverage that big platform to drive hikers from that site to comehike. But I didn't do that due to my inexperience then. I didn't realize how effective that might have been.

Note: You may be wondering whether this was a viable business at all, since meetup.com already had many hiking groups on it and was dominant in the space. Meetup is a loved site, and a very strong community site. It was going to be extremely difficult to compete with it even in the most favorable of circumstances. If that is something you are wondering at this point, then you are right. But we are just getting started with the comehike case study. There are many more points to learn from that are coming up.

Growing An Event Series

I knew that as one of my marketing strategies, I had to get people hiking and organizing their own group hikes on comehike. So I was persistent in trying to get people to hike with me, and raise buzz about the site. But my hikes were regular hikes, and they didn't get any attention or much interest from anyone.

Then one day, I got advice from a very experienced marketer. He told me to make my hikes stand out. He said to do something very unique, maybe even risky or illegal just to get attention, and get press coverage. I never did anything illegal, and his advice stumped me at first. I was hoping he would share a particular tactic that was effective, or some insider suggestion for something I could do to get attention for my website. So at first I wasn't too thrilled with his advice. But in hindsight I realize that he essentially suggested to me to come up with a purple cow concept. Do you remember the section of this book about the purple cow?

At this point, to think about what the purple cow concept may be for any marketing strategy is a second nature line of thinking. But when I was originally given this advice, it was a pretty new idea to me. And admittedly, it stumped me.

I went home, and started thinking about what the purple cow should be for the hiking events. At that time I lived in San Francisco, and I knew that there were some old ships that crashed on the rocks on San Francisco's bay, and you could still see a few of the shipwrecks peeking out of the water during low tide. But where were these shipwrecks? I started doing my research. Eventually found three of the shipwrecks. Then I schedules a hike on my website called "Shipwreck hunt hike during low tide."

Remember the theme of the importance of catchy titles? Judging from that event title alone, this was probably the coolest event going on in the entire city that day. And if it wasn't the coolest (it is a matter of taste), it was certainly one of the most interesting and unique events that day in the entire city.

At that point I had also been trying to leverage local event websites. Typically they drove very few people to my hikes. But that was still more than any other source of hike attendees at that point. Leading up to that first "shipwreck hike" I didn't see many signals that were out of the ordinary. I thought there were just a few people who were going to show up because that was how many people registered for the hike on comehike. But I was in for a big surprise.

I arrived to the meeting point of the hike about 20 minutes before starting time because that was what I usually did as the organizer of the event. Typically, twenty minutes before the event there would be no one there except me. But this time there was a crowd of about 25 people. At first I thought that they were there for another event because I didn't expect that many people to attend my hike, let alone be there twenty minutes early. I went up to the crowd and asked them whether they were all there for an event, and they told me that they were there for a shipwreck hike about which they read in the Sunday section of the largest newspaper in the city.

There is another aha! moment here. Let's explore it. Because the title of the event was so catchy, and the event itself seemed so intriguing, the editors of the Sunday paper who scour the web for interesting events, found my hike, and naturally featured my event because it was going to be interesting for the readers of their newspaper. I wasn't even aware of this since the newspaper is an offline publication, and there was no web traffic that actually went to my site. The newspaper just printed the meeting point of the event, and everyone showed up.

In total there seemed to be 200 people who eventually came to the hike that day. After all those hikes which almost no one attended, it was an incredibly pleasant surprise, but it was admittedly intimidating. Before we had set off on the hike, all the attendees seemed to circle around me in many rows, one after another, asking me many questions that I wasn't answering fast enough before other questions were coming. There were just too many people who I now had to take with me on a trail that was at best wide enough for 2 people at a time. The hike itself was a bit of a disaster because there was just too many people to manage. Being at the front of the group, I had no idea what was happening behind me.

But after that, I never had a poorly attended hike ever again! I had figured out the formula to get good exposure for my events!

Since I couldn't do the shipwreck-themed hike every day (it was so effective that I would if I could) I had to come up with many other intriguing event themes to different historical spots, nature spots, hill climbs, and spots with beautiful views of nature or the city. There were also social components like going to a bar after the hike and socializing. I had come up with enough themes to mix up the events so that the event themes would not repeat too often, and I was able to have a well-attended event whenever I wanted.

That helped my comehike's membership grow. Plus, eventually I had established relationships with every editor of every event website in the city. They liked my events, and supported my venture. They knew to promote my events as soon as they saw them posted.

At this point there was an inflection point in the growth of the business. Since I was putting on many events, and all local event websites were linking to my site, and there was a reasonable amount of basic social sharing, I noticed that the SEO for comehike was beginning to work better and better. All the links from those high-quality websites made comehike very strong in terms of SEO and getting individual pages to rank well. As soon as I would create a new page, it would rank reasonably well in Google search results. But the problem was that I could only write a limited number of pages since I had to do many other tasks like improving the website, promoting and organizing the events, and so on.

Now the challenge I had to overcome was to figure out how to scale up my content production because the more pages the site would have, the more of these pages would rank in Google, and the more leads would come to my site from those Google searches. And, of course, each of these pages had ads on it so more pages meant more revenue.

Here is the advanced tactic I used to scale up my SEO. I looked up a database of all the parks in the world, and imported it into the comehike database. Then I took a database of every city, state and country in the world, and imported that into comehike database. Then I did the same thing with wildlife. I took databases of every animal, bird, and type of tree in the world, and imported those into comehike's database. That gave me hundreds of thousands of records in my database, all having something to do with outdoors or wildlife. Then, since I had all these records in my databases, with one script, I was able to auto-generate a web page for each of the records in the database.

Overnight, my website got hundreds of thousands of new pages. And because my site was authoritative in SEO due to all the inbound links it had been generating from the event sites, in a matter of days, many of those new pages began ranking well in Google search for their keywords.

For a while this created an amazing situation for me. Every day, more and more of my pages were ranking in Google. And each page was generating revenue from Google ads that I put on it. Plus each of those pages has a small conversion rate of getting people to join or organize hikes.

Finally, it seemed that everything had come together, and there was going to be a clear path to scalable growth.

But one morning, as I checked my GoogleAnalytics to get a sense of the traffic from the day before, my heart skipped a beat. From what was previously a beautiful chart that was pointing up and to the right, I saw an absolute cliff. My site had been penalized for having many pages with thin content on them. This was Google's Panda penalty. Do you remember the Panda penalty from the chapter about SEO?

This penalty had put me in a situation where I could no longer rely on SEO, and it made all my future efforts difficult to scale. Overnight, the business went from having a clear growth strategy that was already in motion, to having absolutely no options for viable growth strategies. And since there was no options for scalable and viable growth strategies, there was really no business. To this day, comehike has not recovered from the Panda penalty, and remains a hobby site of mine that I seldom update. It still earns a tiny bit of revenue, but it is not even close to what it could have become. The Panda penalty effectively destroyed comehike.

Keep this example in mind when you try to scale your SEO. Don't go for the near-term risky strategies. The risks outweigh rewards. So be careful.

iv. Your company's case study

Every company is different, and should be marketed differently. Yet this section of the book is where you and I try to craft a marketing strategy for you that is not simply good, but has the potential to be truly great. My goal with this book is to help you create a marketing plan and strategy that should generate great results for your business. Let's get started.

Identify Your Target Market And Find Ways To Get To Know Them Better Than They Know Themselves

Even before you start your business, during the planning stage, you must identify your target market. As you start and grow your business you must get an increasingly better sense for your target market. You should ultimately get to know your target market better than they know themselves. Everything about how you build your business, your product, and how you market your business should keep your target consumers in mind.

Start With Things That Do Not Scale

I realize that every business owner wants to grow their business as much as possible as soon as possible. And in this book, we cover many ways to do that. But notice that in every case study we covered, in the beginning of the growth stages of that business, there was a large part of the marketing strategy that was not scalable, which later became the foundation for the growth of the business.

With Problemio, I answered questions for free, right on my apps. With Comehike, I organized and led hikes. And in the case of HakaLabs, the founders focused on creating a successful event series which put them in the middle of their entire target market.

In each of these cases, these marketing techniques that were not initially scalable, gave the business founders an opportunity to come close to their customers, and interact with them. And that is necessary because no matter how much you think you know about your target market, once you interact with them, you also learn just how much you didn't quite realize about them. And you will learn a tremendous amount more about them and their needs if you spend the time to get to know them.

Your Social Media Marketing Strategy

Once you truly have a great sense about your target market, and the overall market in which you are in, you can begin to establish a long-term strategy for your social media presence. As we covered in our chapter about social media marketing, to reach great scale, you should strongly consider focusing on the media component of social media marketing, and begin to establish yourself and your business as respected voices in your business niche.

Having a presence on the media channels like YouTube and podcasts is great. A part of your company's strategy should also be to establish the business and your personal brand as authoritative in the business niche. The reason it is also important to establish the CEO or founder of the business as a thought leader is that your customers don't typically like to establish personal relationships with brands. People establish relationships with people. And that is why your brand should be as personal as possible.

Your SEO strategy

If you execute on your social media strategy, you should generate a good amount of inbound links and social signals which will be taken as positive signals about your site in the eyes of Google's search algorithm.

Additionally, if you get press coverage on bigger sites, their links to your site in addition to the inbound links you generate from your social media marketing should be enough of an off-site SEO strategy, and to ultimately give your website domain authority in the eyes of Google.

When it comes to your on-site SEO strategy, make sure you produce high-quality content. Don't exchange the pace of content production for quality. Have a reasonably high bar of quality and don't compromise quality for quantity. Quality is more important. But also, don't completely forget quantity. Every new page you create can put you in a position to rank for whatever search term that page targets in Google. The more pages you ultimately have, the more chances you have to rank in Google, and the more people you can drive to your website.

Keep in mind, Google SEO is a long-term strategy. As shown in the Problemio case study, you can get search traffic from other search platforms much faster. So keep an open mind to those types of opportunities.

Your Product Quality

This entire book was spent on strategies to acquire new customers. To implement even half of the suggestions in this book requires a relatively long time, with serious resources devoted to executing these strategies. Yet there is one point I must make before the book is done. In all the excitement about marketing and promoting your business, do not forget about putting resources into constantly improving product quality. Without product quality, generating sales will be difficult, and ensuring that your customers stay, and remain your customers will be even more difficult. Additionally, product design and the design of your marketing materials is also important. As you saw in the Problemio case study, just changing the quality of the app icon to a more professional one, helped to increase downloads by 15%.

v. How to reach a million people

You may have been wondering when we will get to the part of the book that covers how exactly we will reach a million people. Well, here we are.

Ultimately, a million should just be a stepping stone that you reach on your way to a larger number. But for now, let's just focus on one million. To reach one million people per year you need to reach an average of 2,748 people each day. That is the number that you get when you divide 1,000,000 by 364 days that are in a year.

How To Count The Number Of People You Reach

On each different platform on which your business has a presence, the counting is slightly different. For example, if one person comes to your website, that counts as one. But if you sell a product on Amazon.com a purchase counts as one person. But the product page has to be seen by many people before someone makes a purchase. Amazon does not share those numbers. But it can sometimes take 50-100 visits to your product page before a single purchase is made. That means that while 50-100 people may learn about your business, we might only count that as one person who made an actual purchase.

As another example, I sell one paid mobile app for every 50 downloads of my free mobile apps. If I made all my apps free, I could explode the number of downloads, but generate less revenue. But if I made all of my apps paid, I would make more money, but significantly decrease the number of downloads. So what would be the right business decision to make?

What does it all mean? It means that we should take large visitor numbers with a grain of salt. For every single sale of a paid product, fifty people may learn about the product. These fifty people would count as fifty visitors to your website if they were on your website, but because you don't see that number on Amazon, you only count one if a sale is made. Ultimately the visitors numbers become quite skewed.

How To Count Press Coverage

If you are a guest on a popular podcast which gets 10,000 downloads per episode, do you count that as having reached 10,000 or zero since that happened on a property which is not yours? You should count the people you reach on other sites. They don't need to all be on your site.

Probably, if you had your own YouTube video, you would count the views as exposure for your business. But if you had a video on someone else's YouTube channel, you would probably not add the views on that video to your total count of how many people you have reached. But it is the same thing.

The Final Math

It is difficult to predict what the results will be for your business, but let me share how I got to reach 2,748 people per day, which is the same as 1,000,000 people per year.

My mobile apps generate between 1,000-2,000 downloads each day. But half of the apps are paid apps, meaning this number could easily be 2000-3000 if I made all my apps free. Nevertheless, let's stick with the 1000-2000 per day figure.

My YouTube channel generates between 500-1000 views per day. But it is growing monthly because my presence there is still relatively new at the time of writing this book. Because I display ads on the videos before the videos start, that discourages many viewers. If I stopped displaying ads, my YouTube channel would have more views. But let's stick with the 500-1000 daily YouTube views figure.

Additionally, just three weeks before writing this book, I

launched my own podcast which I expect to get about 100-200 downloads per day once it begins to get traction in iTunes and Stitcher.

There are also my two websites, glowingstart.com and problemio.com which together draw about 200 visitors per day. Surprisingly small number relative to all the other platforms, isn't it?

My books give me exposure on Amazon.com but I have no way of knowing how many people actually learn about my business from Amazon.

Now let's focus on the press coverage for my business. I actively answer HARO and RadioGuestList.com queries, which gets me exposure on various blogs, publications and podcasts. In 2013 I appeared as a guest on approximately 25-30 different podcasts and live radio shows. I estimate that the total exposure from the podcasts and websites that cover my business was about 100,000 people.

Additionally, I am a regular writer and contributor on business and marketing for two large websites: websitemgazine.com and 24.com. These sites generate 3,000-10,000 views per article that I write for those publications.

Despite some of the accounting being difficult to track, all that adds up to approximately 2,748 people per day.

Part 7: FURTHER RESOURCES

I want to leave you with a few further resources. Here are most of my business apps for iOS, Android and the Kindle:
http://www.problemio.com

Here is my blog:
http://www.glowingstart.com

Here is my YouTube channel with over 300 business tutorials. I add new videos every day:
https://www.youtube.com/user/Okudjavavich

Here is a tutorial for how to set up your blog on your own in under one day:
http://www.problemio.com/website.html

Here is how my business coaching practice works:
http://glowingstart.com/hire-business-coach-mentor-advisor/

Here are my online business courses on many topics in starting a business, marketing and making money:
https://www.udemy.com/u/alexgenadinik/

ABOUT THE AUTHOR

Alex Genadinik is a software engineer, an entrepreneur, and a marketer. Alex is the creator of the Problemio.com business apps which are some of the top mobile apps for planning and starting a business with 300,000 downloads across iOS, Android and Kindle. Alex has a B.S in Computer Science from San Jose State University.

www.ingramcontent.com/pod-product-compliance
Lightning Source LLC
Chambersburg PA
CBHW051806170526
45167CB00005B/1906